Yates®

GARDEN
PROBLEM
SOLVER

A visual guide to easy diagnosis
and practical remedies

HarperCollins*Publishers*

Visit the Yates website at:
www.yates.co.nz

HarperCollins*Publishers*

First published 1990 as *Yates Garden Doctor*
New editions published 2000 and 2006 as *Yates Garden Problem Solver*
This edition first published 2012 (text revised and updated by Denise Cleverley;
illustrations revised and updated by Deborah Hinde)
by HarperCollins*Publishers (New Zealand) Limited*
PO Box 1, Shortland Street, Auckland 1140

HarperCollins*Publishers*
31 View Road, Glenfield, Auckland 0627, New Zealand
Level 13, 201 Elizabeth Street, Sydney, NSW 2000, Australia
A 53, Sector 57, Noida, UP, India
77–85 Fulham Palace Road, London W6 8JB, United Kingdom
2 Bloor Street East, 20th floor, Toronto, Ontario M4W 1A8, Canada
10 East 53rd Street, New York, NY 10022, USA

National Library of New Zealand Cataloguing-in-Publication Data
Yates garden problem solver : a visual guide to
easy diagnosis and practical remedies.
Previous ed.: 2006.
Includes index.
ISBN 978-1-86950-981-1
1. Plant diseases—Handbooks, manuals, etc. 2. Garden pests—
Handbooks, manuals, etc. I. Orica (Firm). Yates.
635.0499—dc 22

ISBN: 978 1 86950 981 1

Cover design and internal typesetting by IslandBridge
Colour reproduction by Graphic Print Group, South Australia
Printed by RR Donnelley, China, on 128gsm Matt Art

CONTENTS

INTRODUCTION

Many garden problems can be eliminated or prevented by paying attention to some key factors before you begin planting. Start by examining physical features of the garden that may require alteration to enhance plant growth. Note the soil type, drainage, prevailing winds, amount of sunshine received and where the shade falls. If necessary, modifications should be made to the site before plants are purchased.

Soil provides anchorage for plants and is the medium in which most plants grow, and they rely on it for nutrients and water. Healthy soil promotes healthy plants. Poorly drained soils can be improved by the installation of drainage coils or by altering the soil by building it up with organic materials such as peat and compost. Raised beds filled with good topsoil make an easy, alternative garden. A combination of lime or gypsum plus plentiful helpings of peat and compost will aid in breaking down clay soils, and the addition of organic material will help improve sandy soils by increasing water and nutrient retention.

Excessively shaded areas may be lightened by trimming surrounding trees. Hot dry areas may require some planting for shade or an irrigation system (best installed after planting has been completed). If the site is windswept, a shelterbelt will improve the survival chances of more delicate species. Preparation of this sort will help your plants achieve maximum health and avoid disappointing — and costly — losses.

Correct plant selection is paramount to success. There is great wisdom in the often-used quote 'the right plant for the right place'. Plants need to be not only healthy from the outset, but also chosen for their ability to grow in the specified area, so select wind-tolerant plants for exposed sites, and moisture-tolerant plants for damp soils. Existing plants should be trimmed, fertilised and sprayed as necessary. Cull any which are not thriving or are of an undesirable appearance. Purchase only vigorously growing and healthy new plants, disregarding those that are root bound, show signs of poor nutrition, or harbour pests or disease.

Once the initial hurdles have been overcome and the garden is planted, sound cultural practices will ensure success. Watering, feeding and grooming are considered to be the keys to a healthy garden. Effective water management is one of the most important factors affecting plant growth. Too little water results in wilting and leaf drop, whilst overwatering can cause root rot and, in turn, collapse of the plant.

5

WATERING

Correct water application is the key to good water management. To make watering easier, arrange your garden so that plants which enjoy similar water requirements are located together. For instance succulents, which enjoy dry conditions, particularly in winter, should be sited away from ferns, which like cool moist soil. Localised alteration of the soil can also help achieve desired water levels. Add plenty of compost and humus to soil in which moisture-loving plants are to be grown — this will help keep the soil moist.

A layer of mulch — peat, granulated bark or compost — 5-10 cm thick will help conserve water and protect surface roots by reducing evaporation from the soil surface. Mulching also helps to reduce weed infestation, which in turn reduces competition for water and nutrients. Irrigation systems, sprinklers and soaker hoses also aid dramatically in correct water management. Irrigation systems are easy to install and can easily be tailored to suit each part of the garden according to its particular water requirements. Remember, though, that a good soaking every 4-5 days during dry periods is of far more benefit than a quick sprinkle every day. Deep watering encourages roots to grow down, anchoring the plant more effectively, keeping the soil (and the roots) cooler and moister for longer and increasing the plant's nutrient-absorbing efficiency.

FEEDING

Feeding is the second most important factor in promoting a healthy garden. All plants need a particular balance of essential elements. If one is in short supply or unavailable, plant vigour and growth will be reduced. During the growing season, the requirements of plants may change. To maximise growth and ensure your plants are able to withstand pests and disease it is important to feed them regularly. The key elements are listed below.

Nitrogen (N)

Essential for protein building, photosynthesis and cell extension, promotes healthy leaf growth.

Phosphorus (P)

Plays an important role in actively dividing plant cells, vital for the healthy development of seedlings, root growth, flowering and the formation of fruit and seeds.

Potassium (K)

Promotes chlorophyll production, which is important for photosynthesis, and plays a vital part in the strengthening of cell walls and movement of water in the plant. It also aids in building the immunity of a plant to pests and disease and improves the quality of fruits, flowers and seeds.

Magnesium (Mg)

Used in the production of chlorophyll.

Sulfur (S)

Forms part of many plant proteins and is used in the production of chlorophyll.

Most plants require fertilising only in early spring when they are coming into their active growth period. Plants such as annuals and roses, which continue to flower throughout the summer, should also be fertilised in early summer. Plants which flower or fruit in winter benefit from a second application in autumn, as they effectively have two periods of active growth — leaf growth in spring, and flower and fruit production in autumn or winter.

GROOMING

Regular grooming of your garden and its plants within will keep you aware of any impending problems, allowing you to halt the spread of pests and diseases before they reach epidemic proportions. Maintaining the garden in a clean and tidy state will prevent many problems.

Removal of 'undesirables' such as weeds and senescent plant tissue is the best way to maintain the garden in a healthy state. Weeds not only compete for nutrients and water, they also provide a hiding place for unwanted pests and diseases. Dead or dying plant tissue may also be a source of infection, so is best removed and placed in the rubbish bin. Ensure your pruning equipment is sharp and that the cut tissue does not become infected. Old flowers or fallen leaves left in the garden can harbour fungi, which can in turn infect healthy tissue. Regular pruning aids airflow through and between plants and is particularly important over the humid summer months. Pruning helps control fungal diseases by reducing the humidity necessary for their survival.

Applying a copper-based spray,

followed a few days later by an oil spray, several times over the winter period, will help control over-wintering fungi and insects, reducing the incidence of these the following season. Regular cultivation of the soil betters the conditions for plant growth by improving drainage, bringing nutrients closer to the root zone and aerating the soil. Cultivation also assists weed control, and should be accompanied by mulching, to aid moisture retention.

SPRAYING

In the event of an outbreak of either a pest or a disease, spraying may be the only available option. It should be remembered that once insects or fungi damage a plant, it is not possible to repair that damaged tissue. Spraying will eliminate or control the pest or disease, but it is likely that the plant will also require extra care to ensure the effects are not long lasting. Extra feeding and/or pruning will aid the plant's recovery.

In order to understand the use of crop protection products, we need to know the types available.

Fungicides control fungal diseases; they fall into three main categories:

- Protectants — a layer of chemicals is deposited on the outside of the plant and prevents fungal spores from germinating.

- Systemic — these enter the plant tissue and move within the plant's system.

- Penetrant — enter into the plant tissue to control disease from within.

Insecticides control insects; they also fall into three main categories:

- Contact — these eliminate any insects they come into contact with at the time of spraying.

- Systemic — these enter the plant tissue and will be consumed by the insect in due course.

- Penetrant — enter into plant tissue and will be consumed by the insect.

The type of insecticide necessary depends on the feeding method of the insect. For both insecticides and fungicides, thorough coverage of the plant, including the undersides of the leaves, is important. You can also purchase combination sprays, which contain both an insecticide and a fungicide.

When using sprays, always read the label thoroughly and follow the directions. Ensure you always:

- Identify what you wish to control;

- Read the label to ensure you have the correct product;

- Only make up the amount needed to do the job;

- Follow label directions with regard to precautions, application rate and withholding periods.

ORGANIC CONTROL

If you prefer not to use sprays, there are a few alternatives available. Firstly, not all sprays are composed of synthetic chemicals. There are several effective organic sprays. Bear in mind that these sprays will need to be applied regularly for the most effective control. It is possible to control some insect pests — such as caterpillars and snails — by regularly inspecting plants for infestation and physically picking off insects. Insect traps are another ideal way to control garden pests. It is possible to buy yellow sticky traps, which attract whitefly, and pheromone traps, which attract male codling moths, thereby lessening the population of this pest. Snail houses could be considered garden ornamentation, but are very effective if placed in moist shady areas where slugs and snails enjoy hiding out. Simply empty out the house for the birds once it is full. Not all of the insects in your garden will cause damage to plants. A good many of them — ladybirds, praying mantis, spiders, predatory mites — actually prey on other insects. These insects will help reduce garden pests, and care should be taken that insecticides are not applied indiscriminately as they will also harm these biological helpers. Plants can also be protected by the use of physical barriers — cloches, shade cloth or glasshouses. Whichever protection system is used, it is important that ventilation and moisture levels are adequately controlled. It is also possible to enclose individual fruits in plastic or paper bags to prevent insect damage during ripening.

Lastly, modern plant breeding has resulted in varieties that have been selected for their high yields, improved health and quality, and resistance to pests and disease. Many new and improved plant varieties and hybrid seeds are available to the home gardener through your local garden retailer. As well as choosing high-quality seeds, seedlings and plants, it is wise to have variety in the species you plant. That way you minimise the chance of insects or microbial diseases reaching plague proportions.

Growing your own seeds can be very cost-effective — providing you get it right! The table below will help you diagnose germination problems.

Soil conditions

Soil too wet

Seeds need to be damp, not wet, for germination. Poorly drained soils may also have a high incidence of soil-borne fungal diseases. Wet soil can be improved with the addition of peat or by sowing seed in a band of BLACK MAGIC SEED-RAISING MIX.

Soil too dry

Maintaining a constant level of moisture during the germination period is vital.

Soil too cold

Cold temperatures result in slow, uneven germination; disease becomes prevalent and seedlings may be injured. Each species has a different optimum temperature for germination. Do not sow summer plants too early, e.g. bean, tomato, sweet corn, pumpkin, melon, cucumber, petunia, portulaca and zinnia.

Depth of seed

Planting too deep

This will result in delayed emergence. Seeds may not be able to grow sufficiently to reach the surface on the limited reserve within the seed. Soil temperature is also lower with increasing depth. As a guide, sow seed to a depth equal to twice the thickness of the seed. Very fine flower seed, e.g. begonia and petunia, is best just pressed into the surface.

Planting seeds too shallow

This may cause seeds to dry out.

Structure of bed

Seed beds too loose

This results in too much air surrounding the seeds; they will not absorb moisture and are likely to dry out.

Seed beds too firm

This prevents oxygen getting to the seed. Drainage is also impeded.

Pests

Presence of soil-borne fungal diseases

Seeds may rot or seedlings topple. Overwatering, poor drainage and lack of ventilation will increase the incidence of these diseases. Sow seeds in BLACK MAGIC SEED-RAISING MIX and ensure containers are clean. Plan a rotation of crops to prevent build-up of soil diseases.

Slugs and snails

During the late autumn, winter and spring, slugs and snails may destroy seedlings as soon as they appear. Bait areas with BLITZEM every 7–10 days, or with BAYSOL every two to three weeks.

Birds, cats, dogs

These are often responsible for destroying seedlings. Cover seed beds with fine-meshed netting.

Insects

Seeds can be damaged or eaten by insects, e.g. springtails or earwigs. Prevent by sowing seed with SOIL INSECT KILLER granules.

Other

Fertiliser burn

Seed in direct contact with fertiliser can be burnt. Fertiliser should be worked into soil several weeks before sowing seed or placed in a band below or beside the seed. Seedlings in the presence of high soluble salts are also more prone to damping-off diseases.

Seed viability and storage

Always use fresh seed. Some seeds, such as parsnip and lettuce, have a short life once the foil packet is opened. Seed deteriorates quickly if stored in a damp place or exposed to high temperatures. Always treat and handle seed with care to prolong its life. As a general guide, once the foil sachet has been opened, the seed should be used within six months.

WEEDS

1 Bamboo

Cut to ground level. Spray vigorously growing regrowth with AMITROLE and PULSE (mixed together), or apply to new spears after cutting off tips.

2 Clover

When in full leaf, spray with WOODY WEEDKILLER.

3 Convolvulus

When in full leaf and actively growing, spray with WOODY WEEDKILLER.

4 Dock

When in full leaf and actively growing, spray with ZERO WEEDSPRAY, AMITROLE or WOODY WEEDKILLER.

5 Fennel

When in full leaf and actively growing, spray with WOODY WEEDKILLER or HYDROCOTYLE KILLER, preferably before flowering.

6 Flax

Spray with WOODY WEEDKILLER. Most effective when sprayed on young growth after cutting back. Add SPRAYFIX or PULSE for improved coverage.

7 Ginger plant

Spray leaves and roots with AMITROLE and SPRAYFIX; may require repeat applications.

8 Gorse

Spray with ROUNDUP and PULSE when in active growth. Good coverage is essential.

Grasses

When in active growth, spray with ROUNDUP or ZERO WEEDSPRAY.

9 Honeysuckle vine

When in full leaf and actively growing, spray with WOODY WEEDKILLER.

1 Ivy

When in full leaf, spray with WOODY WEEDKILLER and PULSE; alternatively, paint liberally on freshly cut stumps.

2 Kikuyu

When in full leaf and actively growing, spray with ROUNDUP or ZERO WEEDSPRAY.

Moss in lawns and paths

Water or spray with SURRENDER. Use a pressure sprayer to achieve good penetration of the moss.

3 Onehunga weed

Spray with PRICKLE WEEDKILLER in spring from October onwards before the plant sets seed.

4 Onion weed

When in full leaf and actively growing, spray with AMITROLE and SPRAYFIX. Repeat applications will be necessary.

5 Oxalis

When in full leaf, spray with HYDROCOTYLE KILLER or ROUNDUP and PULSE. Repeat applications will be necessary to capture detached bulbils from the mother plant as they grow.

6 Paspalum

When in full leaf, spray with ROUNDUP or ZERO WEEDSPRAY or use a ZERO WEEDING BRUSH.

7 Periwinkle

When in full leaf, spray with AMITROLE or WOODY WEEDKILLER.

8 Privet

Cut down and apply WOODY WEEDKILLER to freshly cut stumps.

9 Wandering Jew

When in full leaf and growing vigorously, spray with HYDROCOTYLE KILLER and PULSE (mixed).

Willow

Cut a frill around the trunk and paint WOODY WEEDKILLER onto the exposed surface. Paint on freshly cut stumps to prevent resprouting.

INSECTS

BENEFICIAL INSECTS

Ground beetle

The ground beetle preys on many harmful insects, and two species have been deliberately introduced to New Zealand as forms of biological control. It is frequently found in litter and debris on the ground, and is most active at night.

Hover fly

Hover flies, so named for their 'hovering' flight manoeuvres, prey mainly on aphids but have been known to feed on caterpillars, mealy bugs and psyllids.

Lacewing

Lacewings and their larvae prey on small, softbodied insects, trapping them and sucking the juices from their bodies.

Ladybird

Almost all ladybirds are beneficial to the health of your garden. Both the adult and the larval forms feed on insects such as aphids, mites, scale and mealybugs.

Praying mantis

The praying mantis feeds entirely on other insects, and as such is a boon to any garden. It frequently lurks in the foliage of shrubbery and scrub, and either waits for passing prey or hunts it down like a cat.

Tiger beetle

Like the ground beetle, the tiger beetle has a wide range of insect prey. It, too, forages in litter and ground debris, but is mostly active during the day. It can run at astonishing speed, and is even capable of catching flying insects.

INSECT PESTS

Aphids

These small soft-bodied insects cluster on young shoots, flower buds or underneath leaves. Control with MAVRIK, SUPER SHIELD, CONFIDOR, NATURE'S WAY INSECT & MITE SPRAY or NATURE'S WAY PYRETHRUM.

Caterpillars

There are many types of caterpillars, which are usually the larval stage of moths or butterflies. Control with MAVRIK, TARGET, SUCCESS NATURALYTE, NATURE'S WAY PYRETHRUM or NATURE'S WAY FRUIT & VEGIE GUN.

Green vegetable bug

The adult green vegetable bug plagues beans, tomatoes, potatoes, sweet corn, vine crops and sunflowers. Control with TOMATO DUST.

Mealybug

These infest citrus trees, ornamentals, container and indoor plants, bulbs in storage and the roots of some plants. Control with CONFIDOR or TARGET.

Mites

The two-spotted mite attacks a wide range of fruit trees, vegetables and ornamentals. Control with MITE KILLER, MAVRIK, SUPER SHIELD or NATURE'S WAY INSECT & MITE SPRAY.

Passion vine hopper

These are damaging both in their adult form and their juvenile form, which is characterised by a white fluffy tail. Control with INSECT GUN or NATURE'S WAY PYRETHRUM.

Scale

Scale insects are characterised by the waxy coating that protects the feeding insect. Control with CONQUEROR OIL, CONFIDOR or BUG OIL.

Thrips

At 1 mm long, thrips are just visible to the naked eye. They disfigure plants and transmit spotted wilt virus. Control with SUPER SHIELD, MAVRIK, CONFIDOR or NATURE'S WAY INSECT & MITE GUN.

Tomato/Potato psyllid (TPP)

Tomato/Potato psyllids are the size of aphids and, under magnification, look like tiny cicadas. Yellow eggs, attached to short stalks can also be seen along leaf margins. Control with MAVRIK.

Weevil

Weevils damage plants by chewing stems and leaves. Control with NATURE'S WAY PYRETHRUM.

White fly

These small, sap-sucking insects attack annuals and vegetables, especially tomato, bean and vine crops. Control with TARGET, MAVRIK, NATURE'S WAY INSECT & MITE SPRAY, INSECT GUN or BUG OIL.

Insects

FLOWERS

AFRICAN VIOLET

1 Yellow leaves

☹ Dry air. Too much sun. Incorrect watering. Overfeeding.

☺ Mist-spray plants. Move to new location. Monitor water and feeding carefully.

2 Pale green leaves with long stems

☹ Too cold.

☺ The minimum temperature should not be less than 15°C. Move pots away from windows on frosty nights.

Crown centre rotten. Limp leaves

☹ Crown rot.

☺ Remove and destroy infected plants. Do not overwater. Avoid temperature fluctuations.

No flowers

☹ Insufficient sunlight. Dry cold air.

☺ Move to new location with more light. If there is excessive leaf growth, remove some leaves to allow light into the crown.

3 Mouldy leaves and flowers

☹ Botrytis or powdery mildew.

☺ Pick off and destroy diseased parts. Spray with BRAVO or GREENGUARD.

4 Straw-coloured patches on leaves

☹ Too much direct sun.

☺ Move to new location.

5 Brown spots on leaves

☹ Water damage.

☺ Keep water away from foliage, and water early in the day.

1 Tiny white insects on undersides of leaves which fly when disturbed

☹ Whitefly.

☺ Spray with NATURE'S WAY HOUSE PLANT or INSECT & MITE SPRAY at three-day intervals, or CONFIDOR AEROSOL.

2 Clusters of white cottony insects

☹ Mealybug.

☺ Wipe off with damp cloth. Spray with NATURE'S WAY HOUSE PLANT or CONFIDOR AEROSOL. If badly infected, destroy plant.

3 Stunted leaves and twisted stems

☹ Mites.

☺ Spray with NATURE'S WAY HOUSE PLANT or INSECT & MITE SPRAY, MAVRIK or MITE KILLER. If badly infected, destroy plant.

ANEMONE AND RANUNCULUS

4 Insects clustered on young leaves

☹ Aphids.

☺ Keep plants well watered in dry conditions. Spray with CONFIDOR, NATURE'S WAY INSECT & MITE SPRAY, MAVRIK, BUG OIL or INSECT GUN at first sign of infection.

5 Leaves yellow and orange-red pustules develop on undersides

☹ Rust.

☺ Spray with SUPER SHIELD, FUNGUS FIGHTER, FUNGUS GUN or LIQUID COPPER.

Bulbs fail to germinate or rot after shooting

☹ Pythium, damping-off.

☺ Disease is most prevalent in cold, wet soils. Prepare soil well before planting, adding organic matter as necessary.

Flowers

ASTER

1 **Plant wilts, yellows and dies.**
   Disease spreads from plant to plant

☹ Fusarium root rot.

☺ Burn plants with symptoms to avoid spread.
   Grow in a different area of garden each year.

2 **Leaves chewed**

☹ Caterpillars.

☺ Spray with MAVRIK, INSECT GUN, SUCCESS
   NATURALYTE, NATURE'S WAY PYRETHRUM or
   CATERPILLAR KILLER.

BEGONIA

3 **Leaves and stems develop soft rots with**
   grey or brown mould

☹ Botrytis, grey mould.

☺ A destructive disease in wet seasons. Remove
   mouldy leaves and badly infected plants.
   Improve ventilation. Spray with GREENGUARD.

4 **Leaves develop spots of white powdery**
   mould spreading over the whole surface

☹ Powdery mildew.

☺ Disease is encouraged by overcrowding and
   lack of soil moisture. Spray with SUPER SHIELD,
   FUNGUS FIGHTER, GREENGUARD, FUNGUS GUN
   or LIQUID COPPER at the first sign of infection.

5 **Leaves become yellow and mottled and**
   plants stunted. Fine webbing present on
   underside of leaf

☹ Mites.

☺ Common in hot dry conditions. Spray with
   MAVRIK, NATURE'S WAY INSECT & MITE SPRAY,
   MITE KILLER or BUG OIL.

CALENDULA

6 **Leaves develop a white powdery mildew**

☹ Powdery mildew.

☺ Spray with SUPER SHIELD, FUNGUS FIGHTER,
   GREENGUARD, FUNGUS GUN or LIQUID COPPER.

CALLA LILY

1 Foliage collapses

☹ Bacterial soft rot of tubers (*Erwinia*).

☺ Avoid planting in wet, heavy soils. Destroy plants with infected tubers.

CARNATION (DIANTHUS)

2 Insects clustered on young leaves or flower buds

☹ Aphids.

☺ Keep plants well watered in dry weather. Spray with CONFIDOR, MAVRIK, SUPER SHIELD, NATURE'S WAY INSECT & MITE SPRAY, BUG OIL or INSECT GUN.

3 Leaves and flower buds with holes eaten

☹ Caterpillars.

☺ Spray with MAVRIK, INSECT GUN, SUCCESS NATURALYTE, NATURE'S WAY PYRETHRUM or CATERPILLAR KILLER.

4 Bud splitting

☹ Sudden and/or great temperature fluctuation. Excess fertiliser and/or water.

☺ Reduce fertiliser and water application to slow growth.

5 Twisted leaves and failure of flower buds to open

☹ Frost or cold snap.

☺ Plant to avoid frosts.

6 Flecking in leaves and/or flowers

☹ Virus.

☺ Destroy plants.

7 Leaves yellow, wilt and die

☹ Fusarium wilt.

☺ Burn plants with symptoms. Plant carnations in different area of garden each year.

Flowers

1 **Red-brown pustules on leaves. Plant becomes stunted**
- ☹ Rust.
- ☺ Most prevalent in warm, humid weather. Spray with FUNGUS FIGHTER, GREENGUARD, FUNGUS GUN or LIQUID COPPER.

2 **Plants wilt and die rapidly**
- ☹ Sclerotinia stem rot.
- ☺ Remove and destroy infected plants. Avoid fluctuations in soil moisture and soils high in organic matter.

CHRYSANTHEMUM

3 **Leaves become silvery or yellow and dehydrated. Minute insects present**
- ☹ Mites.
- ☺ Most prevalent in warm weather. Spray with MAVRIK, NATURE'S WAY INSECT & MITE SPRAY, MITE KILLER or BUG OIL.

4 **White pustules on undersides of leaves**
- ☹ White rust.
- ☺ Remove diseased leaves. Most common in moist weather. Spray with BRAVO or SUPER SHIELD.

Plants wilt and die
- ☹ Fusarium or sclerotinia root rots.
- ☺ Burn plants with symptoms. Plant in different area of garden each year.

5 **Plants wilt. Leaves pucker and distort. Insects under leaves or on new growth**
- ☹ Aphids.
- ☺ Spray with CONFIDOR, MAVRIK, SUPER SHIELD, NATURE'S WAY INSECT & MITE SPRAY or INSECT GUN.

6 **Leaves develop black or brown patches, starting with lower leaves. Defoliation can occur**
- ☹ Nematodes (eelworm).
- ☺ Plant in different area of garden each year.

1 White, powdery mould on leaves

☹ Powdery mildew.

☺ Most prevalent in hot weather. Spray with SUPER SHIELD, GREENGUARD, FUNGUS FIGHTER, FUNGUS GUN or LIQUID COPPER at first sign of infection.

2 Leaves develop yellow spots. Orange or red pustules on undersides of leaves

☹ Brown rust.

☺ Remove and destroy diseased parts of plants. Spray with SUPER SHIELD, GREENGUARD, FUNGUS FIGHTER, FUNGUS GUN or LIQUID COPPER.

3 Pale or dark brown-black spots on leaves. Leaves may fall prematurely

☹ Leaf spot.

☺ Disease is worse in wet weather. Spray with GREENGUARD, FUNGUS FIGHTER, FUNGUS GUN or LIQUID COPPER.

CINERARIA

4 Leaves chewed and eaten

☹ Caterpillars.

☺ Spray with MAVRIK, INSECT GUN, SUCCESS NATURALYTE, NATURE'S WAY PYRETHRUM or CATERPILLAR KILLER.

5 Thin meandering lines through leaves

☹ Leafminer.

☺ Control weeds, which harbour pests. Spray with TARGET.

6 White powdery mould on leaves

☹ Powdery mildew.

☺ Spray with SUPER SHIELD, GREENGUARD, FUNGUS FIGHTER, FUNGUS GUN or LIQUID COPPER. Disease establishes in conditions of high humidity.

CYCLAMEN

1 Leaves and stems develop soft, furry rot with grey-brown mould

☹ Botrytis, grey mould.

☺ Improve ventilation. Do not overwater or water leaves and stems. Remove infected leaves promptly. Spray with BRAVO or GREENGUARD.

2 Foliage droops

☹ Lack of moisture.

☺ Keep plants out of strong sun or heat. Mist-spray foliage in dry conditions.

3 Yellow foliage

☹ Too hot and/or dry.

☺ Avoid extreme temperatures and underwatering.

4 Plant collapses

☹ Overwatering, causing crown rot.

☺ Never let water stand on fleshy crown.

5 Twisted, stunted leaves. Flower buds wither

☹ Mites.

☺ More prevalent in warm weather. Spray with NATURE'S WAY INSECT & MITE SPRAY or GUN, MAVRIK, MITE KILLER or BUG OIL.

Short flowering period

☹ Too warm, too dry. Lack of fertiliser.

☺ Feed with THRIVE FLOWER & FRUIT and water regularly during growing and flowering period.

DAFFODIL AND JONQUIL (NARCISSI)

6 Larvae burrowing in bulbs, which fail to grow. Infected bulbs feel light and soft

☹ Bulb fly.

☺ Destroy infested bulbs. After foliage has died down, cultivate soil to ensure top of bulb is covered and not exposed. Add extra soil if necessary.

1 **Mottling, yellow-brown streaks**
☹ Virus.
☺ Destroy infected plants.

2 **Twisted leaves with ridges**
☹ Nematodes.
☺ Destroy infected bulbs. Plant in different area of garden.

DAHLIA

3 **Holes in leaves and flower buds**
☹ Caterpillars.
☺ Spray with MAVRIK, INSECT GUN, SUCCESS NATURALYTE, NATURE'S WAY PYRETHRUM or CATERPILLAR KILLER.

4 **Leaves develop spots of white powdery mould, which spreads over the whole surface**
☹ Powdery mildew.
☺ Most prevalent in hot, dry weather. Spray with SUPER SHIELD, GREENGUARD, FUNGUS FIGHTER, FUNGUS GUN or LIQUID COPPER.

Stems or whole plants wilt and collapse
☹ Verticillium root and stem rot.
☺ Remove and burn infected plants. Improve drainage to reduce chance of infection or plant in different area of garden.

5 **Flowers and foliage nibbled**
☹ Earwigs.
☺ Clean up leaf litter and other debris on ground. Spray with NATURE'S WAY PYRETHRUM.

Soft, weak leaves, reduced flowering
☹ Excess nitrogen fertiliser.
☺ Use a balanced fertiliser, e.g. THRIVE ALL PURPOSE PLANT FOOD or DYNAMIC LIFTER PLUS FLOWER FOOD.

1 **Yellow-green spots on leaves**

☹ Leaf spot.

☺ Worse in cool, humid weather. Spray with FUNGUS FIGHTER, GREENGUARD, FUNGUS GUN or LIQUID COPPER.

2 **Leaves yellow (stippled or mottled), becoming dehydrated. Fine webbing present on underside of leaves**

☹ Mites.

☺ Spray with MAVRIK, NATURE'S WAY INSECT & MITE SPRAY or GUN, SUPER SHIELD, MITE KILLER or BUG OIL.

DAYLILY

3 **Leaves and flower stalks develop water-soaked spots that expand into raised brown or orange pustules**

☹ Rust

☺ Cut and dispose of infected foliage. Spray new growth at 7-day intervals, alternating with FUNGUS FIGHTER and BRAVO.

DELPHINIUM

4 **Plant wilts. Leaves pucker and distort. Insects under leaves or on new growth**

☹ Aphids.

☺ Keep plants well watered in dry weather. Spray with MAVRIK, SUPER SHIELD, CONFIDOR, NATURE'S WAY INSECT & MITE SPRAY, INSECT GUN or BUG OIL.

5 **Leaves develop spots of white mould**

☹ Powdery mildew.

☺ Most common in hot, dry weather. Spray with SUPER SHIELD, GREENGUARD, FUNGUS FIGHTER, FUNGUS GUN or LIQUID COPPER.

GERANIUM (PELARGONIUM)

1 Small, pale green spots on upper leaf surface, with brown spores on lower leaf

☹ Rust.

☺ Remove infected leaves. Spray with SUPER SHIELD, GREENGUARD, FUNGUS FIGHTER, FUNGUS GUN or LIQUID COPPER. Do not apply excessive quantities of nitrogen.

2 Brown sunken spots. Leaves yellow, fall

☹ Leaf spot.

☺ Favoured by warm, wet weather. Remove infected leaves promptly. Avoid overhead watering. Spray with FUNGUS FIGHTER, GREENGUARD, FUNGUS GUN or LIQUID COPPER.

3 Flowers become spotted and then rot

☹ Botrytis, grey mould.

☺ Most common when weather is wet or humid. Remove infected parts. Spray with LIQUID COPPER or GREENGUARD.

4 Chewed leaves

☹ Caterpillars.

☺ Spray with MAVRIK, INSECT GUN, SUCCESS NATURALYTE, NATURE'S WAY PYRETHRUM or CATERPILLAR KILLER.

5 Wilting of plant. Leaves puckered and distorted. Insects under leaves or on new growth

☹ Aphids.

☺ Spray with MAVRIK, SUPER SHIELD, CONFIDOR, NATURE'S WAY PYRETHRUM or INSECT & MITE SPRAY, BUG OIL or INSECT GUN.

6 Upper leaf surface speckled with yellow blotches. Leaves fall prematurely

☹ Mites.

☺ Spray with MAVRIK, SUPER SHIELD, NATURE'S WAY INSECT & MITE SPRAY or GUN, MITE KILLER or BUG OIL.

Flowers

1 **Undersides of leaves covered with tiny white insects, which fly when disturbed**
☹ Whitefly.
☺ Spray with CONFIDOR, SUPER SHIELD, TARGET, MAVRIK, NATURE'S WAY INSECT & MITE SPRAY or GUN, BUG OIL or INSECT GUN at first sign of infection, and then at regular intervals.

2 **Stunting of plant, yellowing leaves**
☹ Nematodes.
☺ Destroy plant. Plant fresh plant in different area of garden.

3 **Yellow, curling leaves**
☹ Virus.
☺ Destroy plant. Control aphids to prevent infection.

GERBERA

4 **Brown spots with purplish ring**
☹ Leaf spot.
☺ Most common in late summer. Spread by wind and rain. Remove diseased material. Spray with FUNGUS FIGHTER, GREENGUARD, FUNGUS GUN or LIQUID COPPER.

5 **Brown, spreading rot**
☹ Sclerotinia.
☺ Improve drainage. Destroy infected plants. Spray with GREENGUARD.

6 **Leaves yellow and die. Plant dies back**
☹ Phytophthora.
☺ Destroy infected plants. Improve drainage or plant in different area of garden.

7 **White pustules appear on lower leaf surfaces**
☹ White rust.
☺ Remove and burn infected leaves. Spray with SUPER SHIELD, GREENGUARD, FUNGUS FIGHTER or FUNGUS GUN.

GLADIOLUS

1 **Dry appearance, silvering on upper sides of leaves, brown streaks on undersides. Flowers distorted and only partially opened, colour-streaked and speckled**

☹ Thrips.

☺ Hot, dry conditions favour this insect. Overhead watering reduces number. Spray with MAVRIK, SUPER SHIELD, CONFIDOR or INSECT GUN. Add SPRAYFIX for improved control.

2 **Flowers, leaves and stems develop watersoaked spots and grey-brown mould**

☹ Botrytis, grey mould.

☺ Destroy diseased plants. Spray with GREENGUARD or LIQUID COPPER.

3 **Brown, pitted patches on corms**

☹ Fusarium rot.

☺ Store in dry, airy place. Dust with sulfur. Avoid planting in wet or diseased soil.

HOLLYHOCK

4 **Tiny white insects under leaves which fly when disturbed**

☹ Whitefly.

☺ Spray regularly with MAVRIK, SUPER SHIELD, CONFIDOR, NATURE'S WAY INSECT & MITE SPRAY or GUN, TARGET, BUG OIL or INSECT GUN.

5 **Leaves yellow (stippled or mottled), becoming dehydrated. Fine webbing on undersides of leaves**

☹ Mites.

☺ Most common in warm weather. Spray with MAVRIK, SUPER SHIELD, MITE KILLER, NATURE'S WAY INSECT & MITE SPRAY or GUN, or BUG OIL.

Flowers

HOUSEPLANTS

Note: Always spray houseplants outdoors on a calm, cloudy day.

1   Wilting of plant. Leaves puckered and distorted. Insects under leaves or on new growth

☹ Aphids.

☺ Keep plants evenly watered over summer. Spray with NATURE'S WAY HOUSEPLANT SPRAY AEROSOL, CONFIDOR AEROSOL, BUG OIL or INSECT GUN.

2   White, cottony or waxy insects on the undersides of leaves and leaf axils. Plants do not thrive

☹ Mealybug.

☺ Control is difficult. If only a few are present, wipe off with a damp cloth. Otherwise spray with NATURE'S WAY HOUSEPLANT SPRAY AEROSOL, CONFIDOR AEROSOL, NATURE'S WAY INSECT & MITE GUN, BUG OIL or INSECT GUN. Discard heavily infested plants.

3   Stems and flowers covered with flattened red, grey or brown scaly bumps

☹ Scale.

☺ Spray with CONFIDOR AEROSOL or READY TO USE GUN, or BUG OIL. Repeat applications may be necessary.

4   Leaves yellow, become stippled and may fall. Fine webbing may be present

☹ Mites.

☺ Most common in warm, dry conditions. Spray with MAVRIK, SUPER SHIELD, MITE KILLER, NATURE'S WAY INSECT & MITE SPRAY or GUN, or BUG OIL at regular intervals.

1 Brown spots on leaves, flowers and sometimes stems. Fuzzy grey growth and rot may be present

☹ Botrytis.

☺ Diseased and dead plant material should be removed promptly, particularly flowers. Avoid splashing water on foliage and growing plants in crowded conditions where the air is damp and still. Spray with GREENGUARD or LIQUID COPPER.

2 Leaves small and pale. Flowers poor or absent. Lower leaves turn yellow, dry and fall. Spindly growth with long spaces between leaves. Variegated leaves turn green

☹ Too little light.

☺ Place in a well-lit position, out of direct sun.

3 Leaves limp. Soft areas may appear. Poor growth. Leaves curl, yellow and wilt. Tips may brown

☹ Too much water.

☺ Repot plant into fresh potting mix and reduce watering (this is particularly important in winter).

4 Leaves curl, brown and fall

☹ Too cold or wet.

☺ Repot plant into fresh potting mix if too wet. Place in a warmer situation (out of direct sun) and reduce watering.

Spindly growth when in good light conditions. Flowers are short lived. Lower leaves wilt, brown and fall

☹ Too hot.

☺ Place in a cooler, but well-lit position.

1 **Pale leaves, weak growth**

☹ Lack of fertiliser.

☺ Feed with NUTRICOTE INDOOR & PATIO fertiliser. Apply THRIVE HOUSE PLANT FOOD, NITROSOL or BIO-GOLD regularly.

2 **Leaves fall after rapid yellowing**

☹ Rapid change in temperature.

☺ Regulate temperature.

3 **Leaf tips brown and shrivelled. Leaf edges yellow. Buds and flowers shrivel and fall**

☹ Dry air.

☺ Mist-spray with water to increase humidity or sit plant on saucer filled with gravel chips and water.

4 **Leaves turn yellow and fall. Brown tips or edges on leaves**

☹ Draughts.

☺ Position away from draughts.

IRIS

5 **Red spots on leaves**

☹ Rust.

☺ Common in warm, humid conditions. Spray with SUPER SHIELD, GREENGUARD, FUNGUS FIGHTER, FUNGUS GUN or LIQUID COPPER.

6 **Brown spots which run together to form large dead areas**

☹ Leaf spot.

☺ Worst in warm, wet weather. Remove infected parts. Spray with FUNGUS FIGHTER, GREENGUARD, FUNGUS GUN or LIQUID COPPER.

1   Yellow streaks on foliage

☹ Virus.

☺ Destroy infected plants.

2   Rotting leaf bases

☹ Bacterial rot.

☺ Destroy infected plants. Improve drainage or plant in different area of garden.

LILY

3   Insects clustered on young leaves, causing distortion

☹ Aphids.

☺ Spray with CONFIDOR, MAVRIK, SUPER SHIELD, BUG OIL or INSECT GUN.

4   Plants wilt and die back. Bulbs rot

☹ Fusarium, rhizoctonia or phytophthora root rots.

☺ Most common in heavy wet soils. Plant only in free-draining soils.

MARIGOLD

5   Browning and decay of the flower

☹ Botrytis, blight.

☺ Pick off and destroy browned flowers. Spray with GREENGUARD or LIQUID COPPER.

6   Lower leaves develop oval, blackish spots

☹ Leaf spot.

☺ Spray with GREENGUARD, FUNGUS FIGHTER, FUNGUS GUN or LIQUID COPPER.

7   Rotting at the crown or roots of plant. Browning of stems and wilting of plants

☹ Root rot. Fusarium or phytophthora wilt.

☺ Most common in heavy wet soils. Plant only in free-draining situations.

Flowers

1 **Yellow or orange pustules on leaves**

☹ Rust.

☺ Common in warm, humid weather. Remove infected plants quickly. Spray with SUPER SHIELD, GREENGUARD, FUNGUS FIGHTER, FUNGUS GUN or LIQUID COPPER.

2 **Leaves yellow (stippled or mottled), becoming dehydrated. Fine webbing present on undersides of leaves**

☹ Mites.

☺ Spray with MAVRIK, SUPER SHIELD, NATURE'S WAY INSECT & MITE SPRAY or GUN, MITE KILLER or BUG OIL.

NEMESIA

3 **Plants wilt and die. Stems rot at ground level**

☹ Fusarium or sclerotinia root rot.

☺ More common in heavy wet soils. Plant only in free-draining situations.

ORCHID

4 **Small insects clustered on new growth**

☹ Aphids.

☺ Keep plants evenly watered. Spray with CONFIDOR, SUPER SHIELD, MAVRIK or NATURE'S WAY INSECT & MITE SPRAY or GUN.

5 **Young leaves or flower buds eaten**

☹ Slugs and snails.

☺ Lay BLITZEM (pellets or granules) or BAYSOL.

6 Yellow or brownish mottling of leaves

☹ Mites, thrips.

☺ Spray with MAVRIK, SUPER SHIELD, or NATURE'S WAY INSECT & MITE SPRAY or GUN.

7 **Whitish, cotton wool-like tufts on leaves and pseudo bulbs**

☹ Mealybug.

☺ Spray with CONFIDOR, NATURE'S WAY HOUSEPLANT SPRAY or INSECT & MITE KILLER GUN.

1 **Black spots**
- ☹ Glomerella.
- ☺ Avoid overhead watering, reduce humidity and improve ventilation. Discard affected plants.

2 **Flowers deformed and semi-transparent patches on leaves**
- ☹ Virus.
- ☺ Destroy affected plants.

3 **Small, brown, flattened scales on leaves and pseudo bulbs. Leaves yellow and stop growing**
- ☹ Scale.
- ☺ Pick off scale to remove small infestations. Spray with CONQUEROR OIL, CONFIDOR or BUG OIL.

4 **Yellow-brown leaves, sometimes with brown, drying patches**
- ☹ Scorching due to lack of shading and proper ventilation during hot weather.
- ☺ Shade in spring and ensure adequate ventilation.

5 **Rot in growing point. Leaf base blackens**
- ☹ Bacterial rot.
- ☺ Avoid overhead watering, reduce humidity and improve ventilation. Destroy infected bulbs.

6 **Flower buds fail to develop properly, usually withering or falling early**
- ☹ Too cold or too hot and dry.
- ☺ Moderate extremes in temperature.

7 **Brown speckling on young leaves, petals**
- ☹ Excessive humidity.
- ☺ Improve ventilation on warm days.

8 **Small yellow leaves; few or no flowers**
- ☹ Nutrient deficiency.
- ☺ Repot into THRIVE ORCHID POTTING MIX. When watering, liquid feed with THRIVE FLOWER & FRUIT PLANT FOOD.

Flowers

PANSY and VIOLA

1 Insects clustered on young leaves

☹ Aphids.

☺ Water regularly in dry weather. Spray with CONFIDOR, MAVRIK, INSECT GUN, or NATURE'S WAY INSECT & MITE SPRAY or GUN.

2 Leaves develop stippled or mottled yellowing and become dehydrated in hot, dry weather

☹ Mites.

☺ Spray with MAVRIK, MITE KILLER, SUPER SHIELD or NATURE'S WAY INSECT & MITE SPRAY or GUN.

3 White, powdery mould on leaves, particularly in summer or autumn

☹ Powdery mildew.

☺ More prevalent in hot, dry weather. Spray with SUPER SHIELD, GREENGUARD, FUNGUS FIGHTER, BRAVO, FUNGUS GUN or LIQUID COPPER.

4 Leaves yellow and develop red pustules underneath

☹ Rust.

☺ Spray with SUPER SHIELD, GREENGUARD, FUNGUS FIGHTER, FUNGUS GUN or LIQUID COPPER.

PETUNIA

A black discolouration and dry rot of crown. Wilting

☹ Crown rot.

☺ Destroy plants. Improve drainage or plant in different area of garden.

5 Plants wilt and die

☹ Sclerotinia or other root rots.

☺ Spray with GREENGUARD. Destroy badly infected plants and plant fresh plants in different area of garden.

6 Spreading white mould on leaves

☹ Powdery mildew.

☺ Spray with SUPER SHIELD, GREENGUARD, FUNGUS FIGHTER, BRAVO, FUNGUS GUN or LIQUID COPPER.

ROSE

1 Tiny green or pink soft-bodied insects on leaves, stems and buds. Flower buds may look deformed and not open properly

☹ Aphids.

☺ Spray with SUPER SHIELD, MAVRIK, CONFIDOR, BUG OIL, INSECT GUN or ROSE GUN ADVANCED.

2 Yellowing speckling of leaves, white webbing underneath, severe leaf drop

☹ Mites.

☺ More common in hot, dry conditions. Spray with SUPER SHIELD, ROSE GUN ADVANCED, MAVRIK, MITE KILLER or BUG OIL at first sign. Spray with CONQUEROR OIL in winter as a preventative.

3 Hard, grey-white, scale-like insects on woody and green stems. Poor growth, pale, dehydrated leaves

☹ Scale.

☺ Prune badly infected stems and burn. Spray and scrub stems with BUG OIL, CONFIDOR or ROSE GUN ADVANCED in summer. Spray with CONQUEROR OIL in winter.

4 Leaves silvery, with distortion and browning of petals. Flower buds deformed and may not open. Flowers have shrivelled petals

☹ Thrips.

☺ Remove infested buds and blooms. As a preventative measure, spray with SUPER SHIELD, MAVRIK, CONFIDOR, INSECT GUN or ROSE GUN ADVANCED when weather is warm and dry.

Flowers

1 **Circular black spots on upper leaf surface. Leaves may drop prematurely. Flowering may decrease. Stems may be infected**

☹ Black spot.

☺ Remove spent flowers, fallen leaves and prunings. From early spring spray every two weeks with SUPER SHIELD, LIQUID COPPER or ROSE GUN ADVANCED, alternating with BRAVO, GREENGUARD or LIQUID COPPER. Particularly prevalent in warm, humid weather. Prune to increase air movement through plants.

2 **Maroon or black blotches, usually confined to the veins. In humid weather a furry growth may appear on undersides**

☹ Downy mildew (symptoms similar to black spot, but usually occurring earlier).

☺ Cool, moist conditions encourage rapid spread. Keep foliage as dry as possible. Spray with BRAVO, GREENGUARD or LIQUID COPPER in spring and autumn.

3 **Yellow patches on upper leaf surface, with orange pustules underneath**

☹ Rust.

☺ Spray with SHIELD, SUPER SHIELD, ROSE GUN ADVANCED or FUNGUS GUN, alternating with GREENGUARD or BRAVO.

4 **New growth appears distorted with whitish grey powder**

☹ Powdery mildew.

☺ Keep plants well watered as disease is favoured by dry root conditions. Spray with SUPER SHIELD, ROSE GUN ADVANCED or FUNGUS GUN, alternating with GREENGUARD or BRAVO.

5 **Silvering of leaves; plants do not thrive**

☹ Silverleaf.

☺ Remove and burn all infected wood on a dry day. Thoroughly sterilise secateurs after pruning infected plants. Seal pruning cuts with BACSEAL PRUNING PAINT.

1 Small, irregular, colourless spots on foliage. Stunted growth. Yellowing most common on older plants
☹ Virus.
☺ Destroy infected plants to prevent spread. Purchase 'High Health' plants.

2 Leaves yellow and/or develop dark purple tones. Leaves are small and drop prematurely. Slow, weak or stunted growth
☹ Lack of fertiliser.
☺ Fertilise regularly with THRIVE ROSE FOOD, ACTICOTE ROSES or DYNAMIC LIFTER PLUS FLOWER FOOD.

SNAPDRAGON

Plants wilt and die. Occurs more in poorly drained, wet soils
☹ Phytophthora, sclerotinia or verticillium root rot.
☺ Improve drainage by incorporating generous quantities of compost. Destroy infected plants.

3 Yellowing of leaves, red pustules under leaves
☹ Rust.
☺ Most common in cool, humid weather. Spray with SUPER SHIELD, GREENGUARD, FUNGUS FIGHTER, FUNGUS GUN or ROSE GUN ADVANCED.

4 Yellowing of leaves with pale pitting or patches. Grey-brown on undersides
☹ Downy mildew.
☺ Spray with FUNGUS FIGHTER, BRAVO or LIQUID COPPER.

5 Brown leaf spots
☹ Leaf spot.
☺ Spray with FUNGUS FIGHTER, GREENGUARD, FUNGUS GUN or LIQUID COPPER.

Flowers

41

STOCK

1 **Plant wilts. Leaves pucker and distort. Insects under leaves or on new growth**

☹ Aphids.

☺ Spray with SUPER SHIELD, MAVRIK, CONFIDOR, NATURE'S WAY INSECT & MITE SPRAY or GUN, BUG OIL or INSECT GUN.

2 **Leaves develop pale, pitted patches or spots with grey mould on undersides. Occurs mainly in spring and autumn**

☹ Downy mildew.

☺ Most serious in cool, humid weather. Spray with BRAVO, GREENGUARD or LIQUID COPPER.

3 **Whitish powder on leaf surface**

☹ Powdery mildew.

☺ Spray with SUPER SHIELD, GREENGUARD, FUNGUS FIGHTER, FUNGUS GUN or ROSE GUN ADVANCED.

4 **Plants fail to grow; wilt and die**

☹ Fusarium, phytophthora or verticillium root rot.

☺ Destroy infected plants. Improve drainage or plant in different area of garden.

SWEET PEA

5 **White, dusty coating on foliage**

☹ Powdery mildew.

☺ Prevalent in hot, dry weather. Spray with SUPER SHIELD, GREENGUARD, FUNGUS FIGHTER, FUNGUS GUN or ROSE GUN ADVANCED.

Poor germination

☹ Pythium.

☺ Avoid planting in cold, damp soils. Add BLACK MAGIC SEED-RAISING MIX to soil when sowing seeds in the garden.

TULIPS

1 Short stems and bulbs fail to flower

☹ Bulbs not sufficiently chilled.

☺ Chill bulbs in fridge for 8 weeks before planting. Plant Darwin Hybrid or species tulips in warmer climates and plant deeper than usual, about 20 cm deep.

2 Small green insects on leaf tips and buds

☹ Aphids.

☺ Spray with CONFIDOR or NATURE'S WAY INSECT & MITE SPRAY.

TREES, SHRUBS
AND LAWNS

AZALEA, CAMELLIA and RHODODENDRON

1 Clusters of insects on young growth

☹ Aphids.

☺ Keep plants watered in dry weather. Spray with MAVRIK, NATURE'S WAY INSECT & MITE SPRAY, CONFIDOR, BUG OIL or INSECT GUN.

2 Yellow speckling of leaves, white webbing on undersides, dry appearance

☹ Mites.

☺ Keep well watered; hose undersides of leaves. Treat with MAVRIK, NATURE'S WAY INSECT & MITE SPRAY, MITE KILLER, BUG OIL or ROSE GUN ADVANCED.

3 Leaves silver, become brittle and dry. Brown-black specks appear on underside of leaves

☹ Thrips.

☺ Control weeds. Overhead watering will reduce numbers. Spray with MAVRIK, CONFIDOR, SUPER SHIELD, INSECT GUN or ROSE GUN ADVANCED.

4 Black, sooty mould on leaves and twigs

☹ Sooty mould.

☺ Sooty mould fungus lives on honeydew secreted from sap-sucking insects, e.g. scale. Control insects with MAVRIK or CONFIDOR.

5 New leaves and flowers are thickened, fleshy, pale green. Thickenings enlarge and become white or pink, with a powdery appearance during wet weather

☹ Leaf gall.

☺ Remove and burn all infected parts.

6 Leaves yellow and/or develop dark purple tone. Slow, stunted growth

☹ Lack of fertiliser.

☺ Fertilise with THRIVE AZALEA, CAMELLIA & RHODODENDRON FOOD in late spring after flowering finishes and just before buds form in autumn.

Yates Garden Problem Solver

1 **Decline in vigour and leaves turn yellow while the veins remain green**

☹ Soil too alkaline, making iron unavailable.

☺ Fertilise with THRIVE AZALEA, CAMELLIA & RHODODENDRON FOOD or SULPHATE OF IRON in spring before new growth starts. Do not lime. Plants in concrete tubs or planted by new paths may have problems.

2 **Long, silvery, grey, dead areas on leaves**

☹ Pestalotiopsis.

☺ Fungus invades areas on leaves that are sunburnt or physically damaged. Avoid damaging leaves in this way.

3 **New shoots die back**

☹ Dieback.

☺ Fungus invades plant through a wound, killing the tissue and forming a canker. Prune off infected parts and seal with BACSEAL PRUNING PAINT.

BOTTLEBRUSH (CALLISTEMON)

4 **Young leaves webbed together with holes and a tatty appearance**

☹ Leaf roller caterpillar.

☺ Spray with TARGET.

5 **Leaves become distorted, tightly rolled, red-brown and brittle**

☹ Thrips.

☺ Damage most obvious in autumn. Spray with CONFIDOR, MAVRIK or SUPER SHIELD.

Small brown discs on stem

☹ Scale.

☺ Spray with CONFIDOR and CONQUEROR OIL mixed together.

BROMELIAD

1 Centre of plant dies, small side plants still alive

☹ Mother plant slowly dies after flowering.

☺ Detach and replant new plants ('pups').

Entire plant dies

☹ Incorrectly planted.

☺ Plant on raised mounds using THRIVE ORCHID POTTING MIX.

CONIFER

2 Leaves webbed together. Presence of a soft woven case, containing a grub-like insect

☹ Case moth.

☺ Spray with SUCCESS NATURALYTE.

Branches of cypress trees die back. Resin oozes from branches

☹ Cypress canker.

☺ Chamaecyparis and Cupressus are susceptible. Remove affected trees; replant other species.

3 Die-back starting on the inner foliage and moving out. Odd branches dying

☹ Phytophthora or sclerotinia root rot.

☺ Improve drainage. Plant resistant species.

FERN

4 Poor growth. Brown scales on fronds

☹ Scale.

☺ Spray with CONFIDOR or half-strength CONQUEROR OIL. Use with caution on tender foliage.

5 Yellowing, limp fronds on indoor ferns

☹ Air too warm and/or incorrect watering.

☺ Place in cooler position and monitor watering more carefully.

1 **Brown tips on fronds**

☹ Dry air or dry soil.

☺ Mist spray indoor ferns regularly and sit on saucer filled with stones and topped with water. Water outdoor ferns regularly.

2 **White, cottony masses**

☹ Mealybug.

☺ Keep plants well watered and well fed with half-strength THRIVE ALL PURPOSE LIQUID PLANT FOOD. Destroy plant if badly infected. Spray with CONFIDOR or half-strength CONQUEROR OIL. Use with caution on tender foliage.

FICUS IN POTS
(ORNAMENTAL FIG, E.G. RUBBER PLANT, TRAILING FIG, WEEPING FIG)

Sudden loss of leaves

☹ Overwatering. Too cold, too dark.

☺ Move to a new location. Water only when surface of potting mix is dry to the touch.

3 **Loss of lower leaves**

☹ Natural ageing process or overwatering.

☺ Reduce watering.

4 **Yellowing leaf edges**

☹ Underfeeding.

☺ Feed regularly with THRIVE ALL PURPOSE, BIO-GOLD or NUTRICOTE INDOOR & PATIO.

5 **Dry, shrivelled leaves**

☹ Exposure to direct sunlight. Air too dry.

☺ Keep out of direct sun. Mist-spray leaves.

6 **Leaves mottled yellow or silvery with brown specks on undersides**

☹ Mites or thrips.

☺ Most prevalent in hot, dry conditions. Spray with MAVRIK, NATURE'S WAY INSECT & MITE SPRAY or GUN, MITE KILLER, SUPER SHIELD, BUG OIL, INSECT GUN or ROSE GUN ADVANCED.

1. **Small brown discs on undersides of leaves. Poor growth**

☹ Scale.

☺ Common in dry conditions. Spray with CONFIDOR or BUG OIL, or wipe with CONQUEROR OIL.

FLAX

2. **Brown or red spots on leaves**

☹ Leaf spot.

☺ Spray with FUNGUS FIGHTER, GREENGUARD or LIQUID COPPER.

3. **Leaf tissue chewed from underside in long strips, exposing the fibre**

☹ Flax caterpillar.

☺ Spray with SUCCESS NATURALYTE or NATURE'S WAY CATERPILLAR KILLER.

4. **Colonies of soft, white or pink scale, usually near the base or lower leaves**

☹ Scale.

☺ Common in dry conditions. Spray with CONFIDOR and CONQUEROR OIL, mixed together, in spring and autumn. Spray must penetrate leaf bases.

FUCHSIA

5. **Plant wilts. Leaves pucker and distort. Insects under leaves or on new growth**

☹ Aphids.

☺ Keep plants well watered in dry weather. Spray with CONFIDOR, MAVRIK or NATURE'S WAY INSECT & MITE SPRAY or GUN.

6. **Leaves silvery and dehydrated. Undersides covered with brown specks**

☹ Thrips.

☺ Spray with CONFIDOR, MAVRIK, SUPER SHIELD or ROSE GUN ADVANCED.

7. **Yellow leaves. Orange or red pustules develop on undersides**

☹ Rust.

☺ Remove infected leaves. Spray with GREENGUARD, FUNGUS FIGHTER, FUNGUS GUN, ROSE GUN ADVANCED or LIQUID COPPER.

GUM (EUCALYPTUS)

1 Young leaves webbed together. Leaves chewed with a tatty appearance

☹ Leaf roller caterpillar.

☺ Spray with TARGET.

2 Leaves eaten and severely damaged. Presence of large blue-green caterpillar

☹ Emperor gum moth.

☺ Spray with MAVRIK, SUPER SHIELD or TARGET.

3 Young trees develop stem and leaf rot with grey mould

☹ Botrytis, grey mould.

☺ Common in wet, humid weather. Spray with BRAVO, GREENGUARD or LIQUID COPPER.

4 Brown or red spots on leaves

☹ Leaf spot.

☺ Spray with FUNGUS FIGHTER, GREENGUARD, FUNGUS GUN or LIQUID COPPER.

HEBE

5 Pale, clearly defined leaf spots

☹ Septoria leaf spot.

☺ Prevalent in wet, humid weather. Spray with BRAVO, GREENGUARD or FUNGUS GUN.

6 Leaves develop yellow areas which spread and turn black

☹ Downy mildew.

☺ Prevalent during wet weather in spring. Spray with BRAVO, GREENGUARD or LIQUID COPPER.

7 Severe blackening, die back, wilting and death of plant

☹ Phytophthora or sclerotinia root rot.

☺ Destroy plant. Improve drainage and plant phytophthora-resistant species or plant in different area of garden.

HYDRANGEA

Flowers change colour

☹ Incorrect soil pH.

☺ Apply GRO-PLUS LIME to pink hydrangeas; HYDRANGEA BLUEING TONIC to blue hydrangeas.

1 Silvering foliage

☹ Thrips.

☺ Most common in dry weather. Keep plants well watered. Spray with CONQUEROR OIL in winter and TARGET or CONFIDOR in summer.

2 Leaves develop patches of white, which spreads rapidly.

☹ Powdery mildew.

☺ Most common in warm, dry conditions. Spray with FUNGUS FIGHTER, BRAVO or NATURE'S WAY FUNGUS SPRAY.

KOWHAI

3 Leaves severely stripped. Presence of bright-green and black caterpillar

☹ Kowhai caterpillar.

☺ Only a problem if the population grows excessively. Spray with MAVRIK, SUPER SHIELD, TARGET, SUCCESS NATURALYTE or NATURE'S WAY CATERPILLAR KILLER.

LAWN

4 Grass ceases to thrive and may die in autumn or early spring. Turf comes out because of root damage

☹ Grass grub.

☺ Most common on sandy or volcanic soils. Apply SOIL INSECT KILLER granules in February when the grubs are young and near the surface. Water in granules thoroughly.

1 Grass ceases to thrive, browns and dies in summer. Both root and crown damage are apparent

☹ Black beetle.

☺ Most common in northern areas with volcanic or sandy soils. Apply SOIL INSECT KILLER in summer.

2 Leaves and crown eaten. Presence of worm-like casts. Caterpillars can be found in vertical burrows in autumn

☹ Porina caterpillar.

☺ Use SOIL INSECT KILLER granules in autumn to control the young caterpillars before they begin to grow.

3 Presence of a large quantity of worm casts causing a muddy surface

☹ Earthworms.

☺ Remove clippings when mowing. Do not lime, but topdress with DYNAMIC LIFTER ORGANIC LAWN FOOD to keep soil acidic.

4 Purplish, circular or irregular patches which turn brown and die

☹ Brown patch.

☺ Aerate lawn by spiking with garden fork.

5 Small patches of 'cobwebs' on turf show up under dewy conditions, then turn brown

☹ Fusarium patch.

☺ Aerate lawn by spiking with garden fork.

6 Mottled patches of grass. Distinctive bright red threads of fungal growth

☹ Red thread.

☺ Fertilise lawn in spring and autumn. Avoid mowing too closely. Spray with GREENGUARD.

Trees, shrubs and lawns

1 Pale grass. Plants collapse in circles

☹ Pythium, damping-off.

☺ Common in new lawns. Do not overseed. Keep seed moist, but avoid overwatering. Do not use nitrogenous fertilisers on new lawns.

2 Rings of dead grass which get larger each year. May have a ring of puff balls associated with them

☹ Fairy rings.

☺ Spray with FUNGUS FIGHTER.

3 Pale green grass with weed dominance

☹ Lack of fertiliser.

☺ Fertilise in spring and autumn with fertiliser blended for lawns, e.g. LAWNMASTER or DYNAMIC LIFTER ORGANIC LAWN FOOD.

4 Weeds

☹ Poor condition.

☺ Fertilise with LAWNMASTER in spring and autumn. Keep evenly watered over summer. Do not mow too closely. Spray with TURFIX LAWN WEED SPRAY or WEED 'N' FEED.

5 Slippery, green patches of moss

☹ Moss.

☺ Improve drainage, aeration and exposure to sunlight. Spray with SURRENDER. Fertilise in spring and autumn.

LEUCADENDRON

6 Plant wilts and dies. Black dieback may be present

☹ Phytophthora root rot.

☺ Plant only in free-draining situations.

7 Plant silvers and ceases to thrive

☹ Silver leaf.

☺ Prune out infected wood on a dry day and burn. Seal wounds with BACSEAL PRUNING PAINT.

MANUKA (LEPTOSPERMUM)

1 **Sooty, black mould covering plant. Dead branches may look as if they have suffered fire damage**

☹ Manuka blight caused by sucking insects, scale and mealybug, producing a honeydew secretion on which the sooty mould grows.

☺ Spray with CONFIDOR and CONQUEROR OIL, mixed together, to control insects.

2 **Leaves webbed together, often eaten or tatty**

☹ Leaf roller caterpillar.

☺ Spray with TARGET or SUCCESS NATURALYTE.

NANDINA

3 **Yellow, poor growth**

☹ Virus.

☺ Purchase plants labelled 'High Health'. Control insects to help prevent infection.

PALM

4 **White, cottony areas on fronds**

☹ Mealybug.

☺ Remove small infestations with a damp cloth. Spray with CONFIDOR.

5 **Small, brown discs attached to leaves and stems or white scaly material on underside of leaves**

☹ Scale.

☺ Prune off infected fronds or destroy badly infected plants. Spray with CONFIDOR.

6 **Leaves brown at tips**

☹ Dry air, underwatering and cold air.

☺ Mist-spray plant, monitor watering and keep plants away from cold draughts.

Trees, shrubs and lawns

1 **Brown leaves**

☹ Overwatering.

☺ Repot into fresh potting mix and monitor watering to keep just moist, not wet.

2 **Brown spots**

☹ Overwatering. Chilling. Hard water.

☺ Repot into fresh potting mix and remove affected foliage. Move to more conducive growing conditions and use rain water.

PHOTINIA

3 **Leaves eaten**

☹ Caterpillars.

☺ Spray with MAVRIK, SUPER SHIELD, TARGET, SUCCESS NATURALYTE or NATURE'S WAY CATERPILLAR KILLER.

4 **Leaves become silvery and dehydrated with brown specks on undersides**

☹ Thrips.

☺ Spray with SUPER SHIELD, MAVRIK or CONFIDOR.

PITTOSPORUM

5 **Small raised lumps on new foliage**

☹ Psyllids.

☺ Spray with MAVRIK.

SUCCULENTS

6 **Holes eaten in leaves**

☹ Slugs and snails.

☺ Apply BLITZEM (granules or pellets) or BAYSOL.

Leaves damaged with tiny holes all over

☹ Hail.

☺ Remove worst-affected foliage. New growth will eventually replace damaged growth.

Plants turn yellow or brown and leaves rot, or plant dies

☹ Soil too wet. Frost damage.

☺ Transplant into free-draining soil or pot into containers using THRIVE CACTI & SUCCULENT POTTING MIX. Plant in frost-free area.

VIREYA RHODODENDRON

1 Leaf tips turn brown

☹ Wind burn. Drying out. Fertiliser burn.

☺ Plant in sheltered position. Water frequently during summer months. Feed with controlled release NUTRICOTE OUTDOOR GARDEN & SHRUB or DYNAMIC LIFTER PLUS FLOWER FOOD.

Plant spindly and fails to flower

☹ Too shaded.

☺ Move to position with morning sun and dappled shade in afternoons.

Plant not thriving

☹ Planted incorrectly.

☺ Plant on top of soil or in shallow basin filled with THRIVE ORCHID POTTING MIX.

VEGETABLES
AND HERBS

ASPARAGUS

1 Plant wilts, yellows and dies

☹ Fusarium or phytophthora root rot.

☺ Worse in heavy wet soils. Plant only healthy crowns in free-draining soils. Plant resistant varieties, e.g. 'Mary Washington'.

BASIL

2 New plants wilt and die off. Failure to germinate

☹ Soil too wet or cold.

☺ Grow in well-drained soil in warm, sheltered area. Sow (or plant) once soil temperature warms up or grow in containers under cover.

Stunted growth

☹ Soil too dry.

☺ Keep well watered. Liquid feed with UPLIFT ORGANIC LIQUID FERTILISER.

3 Small green insects covering stems and leaves

☹ Aphids.

☺ Spray with NATURE'S WAY PYRETHRUM or INSECT & MITE SPRAY.

Tough leaves

☹ Plants growing too slowly or getting too old.

☺ Trim plants by half and pick leaves frequently to promote tender new growth. Liquid feed with UPLIFT ORGANIC LIQUID FERTILISER.

4 Holes in leaves

☹ Caterpillars.

☺ Spray with NATURE'S WAY CATERPILLAR KILLER.

5 Slime trails and holes in leaves

☹ Slugs and snails.

☺ Apply BLITZEM (pellets or granules) or BAYSOL.

BEAN — DWARF AND CLIMBING

1 Holes in bean pods

☹ Tomato fruit worm.

☺ Protect young plants by spraying with TARGET.

2 Circular, yellow spots on leaves and stems

☹ Rust.

☺ Infection favoured by cool, damp weather. Remove badly infected plants and destroy. Use rust-tolerant varieties. Spray with NATURE'S WAY FUNGUS SPRAY.

3 Leaves eaten mainly on undersides. Leaves and pods rough

☹ Looper or other caterpillars. Vegetable or shield bug.

☺ Protect young plants by spraying with TARGET, NATURE'S WAY CATERPILLAR KILLER, or applying DERRIS DUST.

Young growing tips deformed with clusters of insects

☹ Aphids.

☺ Keep plants well watered in dry weather. Spray with TARGET, NATURE'S WAY INSECT & MITE SPRAY or NATURE'S WAY PYRETHRUM.

Failure of plants to emerge or weak distorted seed leaves

☹ Springtails, bean aphid.

☺ Common in warm weather in late spring and early summer. Spray emerging seedlings with NATURE'S WAY INSECT & MITE SPRAY.

4 Brown spots on leaves, leaf veins become black

☹ Anthracnose (circular sunken spots).

☺ Do not plant beans for at least two years in an area where the disease has occurred. Remove diseased plants and destroy.

1 **Undersides of leaves covered with tiny white insects which fly when disturbed**

☹ Whitefly.

☺ Spray with TARGET or NATURE'S WAY INSECT & MITE SPRAY at first sign and then at regular intervals to eliminate the adults as they appear.

2 **Leaves yellow (stippled or mottled) becoming dehydrated. Fine webbing present on undersides of leaves**

☹ Mites.

☺ Spray with MITE KILLER or NATURE'S WAY INSECT & MITE SPRAY.

3 **Leaves, stems and pods develop soft, rotting areas with dusty grey mould**

☹ Botrytis, grey mould.

☺ Prevalent in wet seasons in poorly drained soils. Remove dead leaves and affected parts. Spray with GREENGUARD.

4 **Cupping and twisting of leaves**

☹ Virus.

☺ Destroy infected plants. Control insects (which transmit virus). Plant resistant varieties.

5 **Leaves, stems and pods develop soft, rotting areas with white mould containing black specks**

☹ Sclerotinia.

☺ Worse in cool, humid conditions. Space plants as far apart as possible. Remove weeds. Improve drainage. Remove diseased plants. Practise crop rotation. Spray with GREENGUARD.

6 **Irregularly shaped lesions, often surrounded by a lighter coloured area or halo. Plants are dwarfed**

☹ Bacterial blight (halo and common).

☺ Wind and rain spread disease quickly. Remove and burn diseased plants at end of season. Practise crop rotation. Spray with CHAMP DP or LIQUID COPPER.

1 Flowers not setting

☹ Very hot and/or windy conditions. Lack of moisture. Excess nitrogen.

☺ Plant French bean varieties in warm climates. Water regularly. Use a balanced fertiliser, e.g. THRIVE ALL PURPOSE PLANT FOOD.

Poor, unthrifty growth and poor seed germination

☹ Soil too cold.

☺ Plant once soil temperature warms to 16°C.

BEETROOT

2 Yellow patches between veins in leaves. Leaves brown and edges roll inwards

☹ Manganese deficiency.

☺ Do not overlime. Apply YATES TRACE ELEMENTS MIX or THRIVE ALL PURPOSE PLANT FOOD.

3 Death of young leaves. Scorched, wilted older leaves. Root flesh has blackened patches

☹ Boron deficiency.

☺ Do not overlime. Apply YATES TRACE ELEMENTS MIX or THRIVE ALL PURPOSE PLANT FOOD.

Bolting, running to seed prematurely

☹ A cold snap (below 10–15°C) followed by a warm spell.

☺ Mulch to reduce soil temperature fluctuations.

White rings, poor colour and texture in roots

☹ Root has overmatured.

☺ Harvest when young.

Poor flavour, roots lacking sweetness

☹ Excess nitrogen.

☺ Use a balanced fertiliser, e.g. THRIVE ALL PURPOSE PLANT FOOD.

Uneven growth

☹ Irregular watering.

☺ Water regularly through dry periods.

1 Light grey spots on older leaves, spreading to other parts of plant

☹ Leaf spot.

☺ More prevalent in warm wet weather. Crop rotation is important. Grow in a different position each year. Spray with NATURE'S WAY FUNGUS FIGHTER.

2 Thin meandering lines through leaves

☹ Leafminer.

☺ Remove affected leaves.

Bleeding when harvesting roots

☹ Top cut too close to crown.

☺ Twist or cut tops 3 cm from crown.

3 Rusty brown spots on older leaves, which spread to younger leaves

☹ Rust.

☺ Remove diseased leaves and destroy. Spray with NATURE'S WAY FUNGUS SPRAY or LIQUID COPPER.

BRASSICA (BORECOLE, BROCCOLI, BRUSSELS SPROUTS, CABBAGE, CAULIFLOWER, SWEDE, TURNIP)

4 Small insects clustered in the developing heart or crown

☹ Aphids.

☺ Keep plants well watered in dry weather. Spray with TARGET or NATURE'S WAY INSECT & MITE SPRAY, or apply DERRIS DUST.

5 Holes in leaves or stems in winter and spring

☹ Slugs and snails.

☺ Lay BLITZEM (pellets or granules) or BAYSOL. Take particular care to protect seedlings.

1 **Holes in leaves in late spring, summer and autumn**

☹ White butterfly and diamondback moth caterpillars.

☺ Protect young plants, rather than older ones. Spray with TARGET, SUCCESS NATURALYTE or NATURE'S WAY CATERPILLAR KILLER, or apply DERRIS DUST.

2 **Undersides of leaves covered with tiny white insects which fly when disturbed**

☹ Whitefly.

☺ Spray with TARGET or NATURE'S WAY INSECT & MITE SPRAY at first sign of infection, then at regular intervals to eliminate adults.

3 **Pale, pitted spots or blotches on leaves. Sometimes downy mould on undersides of leaves**

☹ Downy mildew.

☺ Space plants to allow good air circulation. Spray with NATURE'S WAY FUNGUS SPRAY or LIQUID COPPER.

4 **Scorching or burning around leaf margins. Soft and poor-quality hearts. Cabbages bluish-green colour**

☹ Potassium deficiency.

☺ Prevalent in sandy soils. Use balanced fertiliser, e.g. THRIVE ALL PURPOSE PLANT FOOD, THRIVE FLOWER & FRUIT or SULPHATE OF POTASH.

5 **Circular infections develop on lower outer leaves and cause premature leaf drop**

☹ Cabbage ring spot.

☺ Practise crop rotation. Remove and burn infected plants. Spray with NATURE'S WAY FUNGUS SPRAY or LIQUID COPPER.

6 **Plants stunted with deformed roots**

☹ Club root.

☺ Lime the soil. Ensure good drainage. Destroy diseased plants. Practise plant rotation. Spray seedlings and adult plants with GREENGUARD.

Vegetables and herbs

1 Yellowing between veins on older leaves

☹ Magnesium deficiency.

☺ Use fertiliser containing magnesium, e.g. THRIVE ALL PURPOSE PLANT FOOD, EPSOM SALTS or DOLOMITE LIME.

2 'Whiptail' leaves, thin and straplike. Plant growth is poor

☹ Molybdenum deficiency.

☺ Apply YATES TRACE ELEMENTS MIX or THRIVE ALL PURPOSE PLANT FOOD. Molybdenum unavailable in very acidic soils — apply lime.

Heartless cabbages

☹ Too little organic matter. Soil too loose when planting. Drought.

☺ Add YATES ORGANIC SOIL CONDITIONER (WORMICAST) and water regularly.

3 Split-headed cabbages

☹ Rain after dry period. Frost.

☺ Water regularly during dry weather. Use frost protection cloth.

4 Loose, fluffy Brussels sprouts

☹ Excess nitrogen in soil. Soil too loose.

☺ Avoid nitrogenous fertilisers and excessive cultivation of soil.

5 Tiny heads on cauliflower or broccoli

☹ Cold weather.

☺ Choose all-year-round varieties or protect with cloche.

Bolting, running prematurely to seed without forming hearts

☹ Cold weather followed by warm spell or a check in growth, i.e. drought, root exposure.

☺ Use slow-bolting varieties. Check suitability of variety for the particular time of year.

6 Discoloured, yellowish cauliflower curds

☹ Direct sunlight or frost.

☺ Protect curds by folding leaves inwards or, with long-leaf varieties, tie the leaves together in the centre. Plant self-protecting varieties, e.g. 'Phenomenal Early'.

Cauliflower curds are soft and fuzzy and begin to break up

☹ Overmature.

☺ Harvest when young.

1 **Hollow stems, browning or lumpiness of cauliflower**

☹ Boron deficiency.

☺ Do not overlime. Apply YATES TRACE ELEMENTS MIX or THRIVE ALL PURPOSE PLANT FOOD.

2 **Browning or brown streaks in flesh of turnips with water-soaked cracks. Bitter taste**

☹ Boron deficiency.

☺ Apply YATES TRACE ELEMENTS MIX to soil before planting.

3 **Split roots of turnips**

☹ Irregular growth from uneven watering.

☺ Water regularly through dry weather.

Turnip roots coarse and stringy

☹ Overmaturity.

☺ Harvest when young and tender.

BROAD BEAN

4 **Young growing tips deformed with clusters of insects**

☹ Aphids.

☺ Keep plants watered in dry weather. Spray with TARGET or NATURE'S WAY INSECT & MITE SPRAY at first sign of infestation.

5 **Dark brown or black spots on leaves**

☹ Chocolate spot, botrytis.

☺ Spray with LIQUID COPPER. Good drainage helps avoid the problem. Space plants to encourage good air circulation. Control weeds.

1 Red or purple raised rust pustules, particularly on undersides of leaves

☹ Rust.

☺ Spray with NATURE'S WAY FUNGUS SPRAY or LIQUID COPPER at first sign of infection.

Distorted leaves and pods

☹ Green vegetable bug.

☺ Apply DERRIS DUST. Insecticides with stronger odour can be detected by the green vegetable bug, which will fly away before the sprays can be effective, only to reinfest the plant later.

Poor fruit set

☹ Too cold at flowering — planted too early.

☺ Plant later to ensure warmer temperatures at fruit set.

CARROT and PARSNIP

2 Leaves are stunted and deformed with clusters of insects

☹ Aphids.

☺ Keep well watered in dry weather. Spray with NATURE'S WAY INSECT & MITE SPRAY or PYRETHRUM.

3 Carrots tunnelled by grubs. Leaves may turn orange

☹ Carrot rust fly.

☺ Place SOIL INSECT KILLER granules in seed row when sowing. Keep tops of carrot roots covered with soil. Rotate crops.

4 Forked and misshapen roots

☹ Stones, clods or lumps of bulky organic manure in soil. Delayed thinning.

☺ Prepare a deep, crumbly, well-drained soil which allows roots to expand and grow quickly. Thin to 2–3 cm apart when carrots are 5 cm high.

Seedlings burn off

☹ Hot sunny weather at tender stage of growth.

☺ Sprinkle with water to keep moist.

1 Excessive leaf growth

☹ Excess nitrogen.

☺ Avoid nitrogenous fertilisers. Use a balanced fertiliser, e.g. THRIVE ALL PURPOSE PLANT FOOD.

2 Green tops of carrot roots

☹ Sunlight on exposed crowns.

☺ Earth up to cover crowns during growth.

3 Carrots pale colour

☹ Pale variety, e.g. 'Egmont Gold'. Strongly acid soil. Excess nitrogen.

☺ Plant deeply coloured varieties, e.g. 'Early Chantenay' or 'Majestic Red'. Lime the soil. Avoid nitrogen fertiliser. Potash increases intensity of colour.

4 Roots cracked or split

☹ Interior grows faster than skin, caused by heavy rain following a dry spell or overfertilising.

☺ Water frequently during dry weather.

Bolting or running to seed prematurely without forming roots

☹ Seedlings subject to snap in cool weather.

☺ Cover with cloche if cold snap forecast.

Poor parsnip germination

☹ Seed is short-lived.

☺ Use fresh parsnip seed each year.

CELERY

5 Clusters of insects on leaves, particularly in the young crown area

☹ Aphids.

☺ Keep well watered in dry weather. Spray with NATURE'S WAY INSECT & MITE SPRAY or PYRETHRUM.

1 **Leaves covered with small black spots, or brown rusty spots on leaves and stems**

☹ Septoria leaf spot.

☺ Most prevalent in cool weather. Use disease-free seed. Practise crop rotation on a seven-year cycle. Spray with BRAVO or LIQUID COPPER.

Bolting or running prematurely to seed

☹ Cold snap followed by a warm spell. Soil drying out.

☺ Water regularly during dry weather.

2 **Thin, dry stalks**

☹ Lack of fertiliser and/or moisture.

☺ Feed and water regularly.

3 **Split stalks**

☹ Dry soil. Excess nitrogen in soil.

☺ Water thoroughly in dry weather. Use a balanced fertiliser, e.g. THRIVE ALL PURPOSE PLANT FOOD.

CHIVES

4 **Small black insects feeding on leaves**

☹ Aphids.

☺ Keep well watered in dry weather. Spray with NATURE'S WAY INSECT & MITE SPRAY or PYRETHRUM.

CUCURBIT (COURGETTE, CUCUMBER, MARROW, MELON, PUMPKIN, ROCK MELON, WATERMELON, ZUCCHINI)

5 **Undersides of leaves covered with tiny white insects which fly when disturbed**

☹ Whitefly.

☺ Control is difficult once a large population has built up. Spray with TARGET, CONFIDOR or NATURE'S WAY INSECT & MITE SPRAY at first sign of infestation, then regularly thereafter.

1 **Leaves yellow (stippled or mottled), becoming dehydrated. Fine webbing present on undersides of leaves**

☹ Mites.

☺ Most severe in warm weather. Spray with MITE KILLER or NATURE'S WAY INSECT & MITE SPRAY.

2 **Flowers and fruit rot in humid conditions**

☹ Botrytis, grey mould.

☺ Prevalent in humid conditions.

3 **Leaves become blotched and yellow, sometimes with mould on undersides**

☹ Downy mildew.

☺ In cool, moist conditions an attack can be severe. Spray with BRAVO, NATURE'S WAY FUNGUS SPRAY or LIQUID COPPER.

4 **White or grey mould on leaves, starting as spots and spreading over the whole leaf**

☹ Powdery mildew.

☺ Most common in warm dry conditions. Spray with NATURE'S WAY FUNGUS SPRAY.

5 **Wilting of leaves**

☹ Large leaves lose moisture quickly in warm weather.

☺ Water frequently and thoroughly. Mulch around plants to conserve soil moisture.

Excessive leaf growth

☹ Excess nitrogen.

☺ Use a balanced fertiliser, e.g. THRIVE ALL PURPOSE PLANT FOOD.

Fruit yellow and bitter to taste

☹ Overmaturity.

☺ Harvest when young.

1 **Water-soaked spots on leaves which dry and crack. Immature fruit may fall**

☹ Leaf spot.

☺ Crop rotation of two years or more is important. Destroy diseased material. Spray with LIQUID COPPER.

2 **Brown-black spots on leaves**

☹ Anthracnose.

☺ Spray with LIQUID COPPER. Do not grow cucurbits in the same soil more than once in every four years. Practise crop rotation and plant resistant cultivars.

Shortage of fruit

☹ Poor pollination caused by absence of bees in dull, cold weather.

☺ Fruit setting improves with warmer weather. Hand pollinate. To keep plants cropping it is necessary to remove fruit as they mature.

3 **Predominance of male flowers**

☹ Under certain stress conditions (poor nutrition, low light, low temperatures, low water) the male flowers of some cultivars become dominant on the plant.

☺ Ensure plants receive adequate nutrition and appropriate water.

4 **Damaged skin with pale, discoloured blotches**

☹ Fruit exposed to wet, damp soil.

☺ Place block of wood or tile under fruits to keep them off damp soil.

Lack of flavour

☹ Harvested before fully ripened.

☺ To test for ripeness:

Watermelon: Skin becomes slightly bumpy on side of fruit in contact with soil.

Rock melon: Stalk comes away from fruit. Fruit develops flavour if kept for two or three days.

EGGPLANT (AUBERGINE)

1 **Small insects on new growth. Leaves wilt and twist**

☹ Aphids.

☺ Keep plants well watered in dry weather. Spray at first sign of infection with TARGET or NATURE'S WAY INSECT & MITE SPRAY.

2 **Distortion of young leaves and silvering of older leaves**

☹ Thrips.

☺ Spray at first sign with CONFIDOR or NATURE'S WAY INSECT & MITE SPRAY.

3 **Leaves chewed**

☹ Caterpillars.

☺ Spray with SUCCESS NATURALYTE or NATURE'S WAY PYRETHRUM or CATERPILLAR KILLER. Alternatively, pick off insects by hand.

4 **Plants wilt and die rapidly**

☹ Sclerotinia.

☺ Destroy infected plants. Avoid fluctuations in watering.

5 **Streaks in foliage**

☹ Virus.

☺ Destroy infected plants. Control aphids and thrips to prevent infection. Plant resistant varieties, e.g. 'Blacknite'.

Poor fruit set

☹ Lack of pollination.

☺ Cool, dull weather and lack of insects. May require hand pollination with a small brush.

KUMARA

6 **Galls on roots. Poor growth**

☹ Nematodes.

☺ Rotate crop so kumara are not grown in the same area more than one year in three.

LETTUCE

1 Insects clustered on leaves

☹ Aphids.

☺ More common in dry weather. Keep plants well watered. Spray with NATURE'S WAY INSECT & MITE SPRAY or PYRETHRUM.

2 Brown spots on leaves

☹ Leaf spot.

☺ Common after cold, wet weather in badly drained situations. Practise crop rotation. Spray with LIQUID COPPER.

3 Soft rot of leaves with grey mould

☹ Botrytis, grey mould.

☺ Prevalent in humid weather. Spreads rapidly. Improve drainage. Keep weeds down. Keep good air movement through canopy. Remove damaged parts. Spray with LIQUID COPPER.

4 Stunting, rotting at ground level; brown slime rot in hearts. Bitterness

☹ Sclerotinia.

☺ Remove affected plants with surrounding soil and destroy. Keep weeds down. Keep good air movement through canopy.

Bolting, running to seed prematurely

☹ Check in growth, i.e. delayed transplanting, overcrowding, dryness, hot weather.

☺ Select right variety for growing in summer and winter. Pay particular attention to soil preparation, watering, and feeding.

Bitterness

☹ Slow growth and/or overmaturity.

☺ Grow quickly in warm soils with plenty of moisture.

Poor seed germination
- ☹ Lack of moisture. Too hot.
- ☺ At 20°C, germination takes 7–10 days. Above 25°C seeds become dormant. Use fresh seed.

Young seedlings eaten
- ☹ Slugs or snails.
- ☺ Protect with BLITZEM (pellets or granules) or BAYSOL.

1   No hearts
- ☹ Shortage of organic matter. Not enough light. Overcrowding. Drought.
- ☺ Incorporate organic matter into soil at planting time, e.g. YATES ORGANIC SOIL CONDITIONER (WORMICAST), BIO GOLD or DYNAMIC LIFTER organic fertiliser. Space plants and keep them watered.

2   'Tipburn', leaf edges turn brown
- ☹ Sudden water loss from leaves during warm spell.
- ☺ Ensure even watering in warm conditions.

ONION (GARLIC, LEEK, SHALLOT)

3   Foliage blotched, silver, grey or white, leaves becoming deformed in severe cases
- ☹ Thrips.
- ☺ Most common in dry weather. Control weeds and keep plants well watered. Spray with NATURE'S WAY FRUIT & VEGIE GUN.

4   Grey or purple spots on leaves. Pitted appearance
- ☹ Downy mildew.
- ☺ More serious in wet weather. Improve soil drainage and air circulation. Spray with NATURE'S WAY FUNGUS SPRAY or LIQUID COPPER.

Vegetables and herbs

75

1 Heavy top growth and drooping leaves

☹ Too much fresh manure or nitrogen in soil.

☺ Work organic matter into the soil thoroughly. Use a balanced fertiliser, e.g. THRIVE ALL PURPOSE PLANT FOOD.

Soft bulbs

☹ Excess nitrogen.

☺ Use balanced fertiliser, e.g. THRIVE ALL PURPOSE PLANT FOOD.

Poor keeping quality

☹ Excessive moisture.

☺ Plant long-keeping variety, e.g. 'Pukekohe Longkeeper'.

2 Thick necks in mature onions

☹ Delay in transplanting of seedling. Sowing too early. Excess nitrogen. Planting too deep. Dry soil in early growth period.

☺ Transplant before seedling stem exceeds 6 mm in width. Use balanced fertiliser, e.g. THRIVE ALL PURPOSE PLANT FOOD. Water regularly in dry weather.

3 Soft rots with grey or brown mould. Common in storage

☹ Botrytis, grey mould.

☺ Store in dry, well-ventilated conditions.

Failing to bulb

☹ Seed sown at wrong time. Excess nitrogen.

☺ Sow early, mid, late season varieties accordingly. Use balanced fertiliser, e.g. THRIVE ALL PURPOSE PLANT FOOD.

4 Bulbs split at base

☹ Heavy rain or watering after a prolonged dry spell.

☺ Water frequently during dry weather.

Bolting, plant runs to seed

☹ Seed sown at wrong time.

☺ Sow early, mid, late season varieties accordingly.

PARSLEY

1 **Wilting of plant. Leaves puckered and distorted. Insects under leaves or on new growth**

☺ Aphids.

☺ Water regularly in dry weather. Spray with NATURE'S WAY INSECT & MITE SPRAY.

2 **Silvering of leaves**

☹ Thrips.

☺ Most common in dry weather. Control weeds and keep well watered.

3 **Spots on leaves**

☹ Leaf spot.

☺ Cut and destroy infected parts. Spray with NATURE'S WAY FUNGUS SPRAY.

PEA

4 **Wilting of plant. Leaves puckered and distorted. Insects under leaves or on new growth**

☹ Aphids.

☺ Water regularly in dry weather. Spray with NATURE'S WAY INSECT & MITE SPRAY or PYRETHRUM.

5 **Leaf surfaces yellow or pitted with grey mould on undersides**

☹ Downy mildew.

☺ Avoid areas with shade or poor air circulation. Spray with NATURE'S WAY FUNGUS SPRAY.

6 **Irregular, dark, water-soaked spots or lesions. Young infected pods shrivel**

☹ Bacterial blight.

☺ More prevalent in cool, damp weather. Spray with NATURE'S WAY FUNGUS SPRAY or LIQUID COPPER. Practise a three-year crop rotation.

Flowers not setting
- ☹ Frosty conditions.
- ☺ Plant to avoid frosts.

1 Plants stunted and yellow
- ☹ Wet soil, poor drainage. Lack of fertiliser.
- ☺ Improve soil conditions and apply a balanced fertiliser, e.g. THRIVE ALL PURPOSE PLANT FOOD.

PEPPER (CAPSICUM)

2 Plant wilts, leaves pucker and distort. Insects under leaves or on new growth
- ☹ Aphids.
- ☺ Water regularly. Spray with NATURE'S WAY INSECT & MITE SPRAY or PYRETHRUM.

3 Leaves become silvery and dehydrated with brown specks on undersides
- ☹ Thrips.
- ☺ Most common in dry weather. Control weeds and keep well watered. Apply DERRIS DUST.

4 Soft, brown rot which develops a white, fluffy growth
- ☹ Sclerotinia.
- ☺ Disease is worse in cool, humid conditions. Practise crop rotation and improve drainage.

5 Streaking of foliage
- ☹ Virus.
- ☺ Control aphids and thrips throughout growing season. Destroy virus-infected plants. Plant resistant varieties, e.g. 'Californian Wonder'.

POTATO

6 Plant wilts, leaves pucker and distort. Insects under leaves or on new growth
- ☹ Aphids.
- ☺ Keep well watered in dry weather. Spray with NATURE'S WAY INSECT & MITE SPRAY or PYRETHRUM.

1 **Blotches and holes in leaves. Tunnels in stems and tubers**
- ☹ Potato tuber moth.
- ☺ Incorporate plenty of organic matter in soil and keep plants well watered to prevent soil cracking that allows moth to reach tubers. Don't plant in warmest months.

2 **Irregular, greenish brown-black patches on leaves and stalks, rapidly enlarging in wet weather. Whole plant becomes blackened**
- ☹ Late blight.
- ☺ Most common in humid conditions with cool nights and warm days. Spray regularly with BRAVO or GREENGUARD.

3 **Small spots on older leaves, increasing to 1 cm in size. Concentric rings can be seen in the spot**
- ☹ Early blight.
- ☺ Common in hot, humid weather. Spray with BRAVO.

4 **Yellow, blotched leaves**
- ☹ Late spring frosts damage shoots.
- ☺ Plant to avoid frosts.

No sprouts on seed tubers
- ☹ Frosting of seed tubers in transit or in storage. Diseased tuber.
- ☺ Keep tubers cool, but do not freeze. Purchase certified virus-free seed potatoes.

Soft and rubbery tubers
- ☹ Dry summer.
- ☺ Water frequently during dry spells.

5 **Spindly sprouts on seed tubers**
- ☹ Keeping tubers too dark or too warm prior to planting.
- ☺ Store seed tubers in well-ventilated, cool position in indirect light.

1 **Stunted plants with distorted growing tips. Edges of curled leaves have pink tinge. Plants develop scorched appearance and collapse prematurely**

☹ Tomato/potato psyllid.

☺ Spray with MAVRIK.

2 **Yellowing and browning of tissue between the veins of leaflets**

☹ Magnesium deficiency.

☺ Apply fertiliser containing magnesium when preparing the soil for planting, e.g. THRIVE ALL PURPOSE PLANT FOOD, or add EPSOM SALTS.

3 **Yellow mottling on leaves. Crinkling of leaf tissue. Plants may die early**

☹ Mosaic virus.

☺ Plant only certified virus-free seed. Control aphids.

Tubers crack and split during growth

☹ Tubers suffered dry spell.

☺ Keep well watered.

Tubers with soapy, waxy texture

☹ Lifting tubers before mature. Excess lime.

☺ For storing potatoes, dig after the top has completely died down. Only apply lime to acidic soils.

4 **Hollow centres in large tubers**

☹ Prolonged wet spell after dry weather.

☺ Keep watered during dry weather.

Tubers with sweet taste

☹ Tubers too cool in storage.

☺ Store in a cool, dark place.

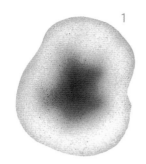

1. **Tubers have black heart or turn black when cooked**
- ☹ Potash deficiency. Stored in too high temperatures (above 10°C).
- ☺ Use a balanced fertiliser, e.g. THRIVE ALL PURPOSE PLANT FOOD. Store in a cool place.

Poor emergence and/or small tubers
- ☹ Sweating of tubers in storage caused by poor ventilation. Tubers stored for over six months.
- ☺ Store carefully. Do not plant too late. Avoid planting in cold, wet soil.

RADISH, SWEDE and TURNIP

2. **Wilting of plant. Leaves puckered and distorted. Insects under leaves or on new growth**
- ☹ Aphids.
- ☺ Keep well watered during dry weather. Spray with NATURE'S WAY PYRETHRUM or INSECT & MITE SPRAY.

3. **Holes in leaves**
- ☹ Caterpillars.
- ☺ Spray with SUCCESS NATURALYTE or NATURE'S WAY CATERPILLAR KILLER.

4. **Irregular, black patches on root**
- ☹ Black root.
- ☺ More common in warm weather and if soil is moist. Improve soil drainage. Practise crop rotation.

5. **Deformed roots**
- ☹ Club root.
- ☺ Lime the soil. Ensure good drainage. Do not grow more than once in seven years in the same area.

SILVERBEET

Seedlings eaten
☹ Slugs or snails.
☺ Protect with BLITZEM pellets or granules.

1 Fine tracings appear on leaves
☹ Silverbeet leafminer.
☺ Remove affected leaves. Expose pupae in soil for birds.

2 Red-brown pustules form on leaves
☹ Rust.
☺ Spray with NATURE'S WAY FUNGUS SPRAY.

3 Chewed foliage
☹ Caterpillars.
☺ Apply DERRIS DUST or spray with SUCCESS NATURALYTE or NATURE'S WAY CATERPILLAR KILLER.

Bolting, running to seed prematurely
☹ Prolonged cold spell followed by warm weather. Transplanting shock.
☺ Sow seed directly into the ground where possible, to avoid transplanting shock.

SPINACH

Bolting, running to seed prematurely
☹ Long days and high temperatures. Check in growth. Lack of water or fertiliser. Overcrowding.
☺ Do not overcrowd plants. Keep well watered in dry weather. Sow 'Summer Supreme' over summer months.

4 Yellow blotches between veins in leaves
☹ Manganese deficiency (common in sandy soils) or soil too alkaline.
☺ Do not overlime. Apply YATES TRACE ELEMENTS MIX. Foliar-feed with THRIVE ALL PURPOSE PLANT FOOD.

SWEET CORN

1 Leaves eaten, tassel eaten and cobs attacked

☹ Corn ear worm.

☺ Control when plants are young. Spray with NATURE'S WAY PYRETHRUM as cobs begin to form.

Galls form on cob

☹ Smut.

☺ Destroy infected plants. Use clean seed.

Tough kernels

☹ Overmature when harvested. Storing cobs too long. Overcooking.

☺ Pick and use cobs when young and fresh. Use new 'Super Sweet' varieties.

2 Poorly filled cob

☹ Poor pollination.

☺ Plant in blocks rather than rows.

Corn eaten at end of cob

☹ Corn ear worm.

☺ Control when plants are young. Spray with NATURE'S WAY PYRETHRUM as cobs begin to form.

TOMATO

3 Split fruit

☹ Heavy watering or rain when temperatures are high.

☺ Water regularly through dry periods.

Blossom drop

☹ Low temperatures in spring or very high temperatures in summer.

☺ Wait until temperatures are warmer in spring. Shade plants in hot weather. Protect plants from wind.

1 **Yellowing and stunted growing tip. Curling leaves. Flowers falling. Fruit small and misshapen**
- ☹ Tomato/potato psyllid.
- ☺ Spray with MAVRIK.

2 **Paper-brown patches on fruit**
- ☹ Sun scald, exposure to bright sunlight.
- ☺ Do not remove too many old leaves at once. Shade plants.

3 **Bottom of fruit sunken, leathery and blackened**
- ☹ Blossom end rot, lack of calcium, together with irregular watering.
- ☺ Most serious when plants are growing rapidly. Apply lime prior to planting. Water daily. Mulch plants to avoid fluctuations in soil temperature and moisture.

4 **Blotchy ripening, parts of fruit remain yellow or orange**
- ☹ Too much heat. Too little potash. Too much water.
- ☺ Water moderately. Feed with THRIVE FLOWER & FRUIT PLANT FOOD or GRO-PLUS TOMATO FOOD.

5 **Misshapen fruit**
- ☹ Virus disease. Poor pollination due to cold weather at flowering or very high temperatures.
- ☺ Plant later in spring.

6 **Small caterpillar tunnel holes in fruit**
- ☹ Tomato fruit worm.
- ☺ Spray with SUCCESS NATURALYTE or apply TOMATO DUST as fruit begin to form.

7 **Green back, area around stalk remains hard, green and unripe**
- ☹ Excess sunlight. Too dry. Too little potash.
- ☺ Apply SULPHATE OF POTASH. Water regularly.

1 Leaves yellow between veins

🙁 Magnesium deficiency.

😊 Feed with THRIVE ALL PURPOSE PLANT FOOD at planting. Foliar feed with NITROSOL TOMATO FOOD.

2 Tiny white insects on undersides of leaves which fly when disturbed

🙁 Whitefly.

😊 Spray with TARGET, CONFIDOR, MAVRIK or NATURE'S WAY INSECT & MITE SPRAY.

3 Leaves yellow (mottled) and dehydrate in hot, dry weather, especially in glasshouses. Minute pests under leaves

🙁 Mites.

😊 Spray with MITE KILLER or NATURES' WAY INSECT & MITE SPRAY.

4 Rolling of older leaves

🙁 Excess deleafing or a wide variation between day and night temperatures.

😊 Mulch plants to control temperature and soil moisture fluctuations.

5 Plant wilts, leaves pucker and distort. Insects under leaves or on new growth

🙁 Aphids.

😊 Apply TOMATO DUST or spray with TARGET, MAVRIK, CONFIDOR or NATURE'S WAY PYRETHRUM.

6 Irregular, brown patches on leaves, spreading rapidly in wet weather

🙁 Late blight.

😊 Serious in cool, humid weather. Prevent by spraying regularly with BRAVO or LIQUID COPPER. Remove affected plants.

7 Small spots on older leaves. Dark mould present

🙁 Early blight.

😊 More common in warm, wet weather. Prevent by spraying regularly with BRAVO or LIQUID COPPER. Remove affected plants.

1 **Leaves, stems and fruit develop a grey-brown rot or mould**

☹ Botrytis, grey mould.

☺ Remove affected parts. Spray with GREENGUARD. Provide adequate spacing and prune to promote ventilation.

2 **Older leaves showing yellow blotches with grey mould on undersides. Young leaves showing pale circular spots**

☹ Leaf mould.

☺ Spray with NATURE'S WAY FUNGUS SPRAY.

3 **Black specks on leaves, often with a yellowish halo. Common in early spring or in cool, wet weather**

☹ Bacterial spot.

☺ Use disease-free seed. Practise four- to five-year crop rotation. Control weeds. Burn diseased plants. Avoid overhead watering. Spray with LIQUID COPPER.

4 **Drying and withering of leaves**

☹ Verticillium wilt, bacterial wilt.

☺ Do not grow in same area more than one year in three. Plant verticillium-resistant varieties, e.g. 'Big Beef', 'Grosse Lisse' and 'Roma'.

5 **Plants suddenly stop growing. Bronze spots develop between leaves. Fruit ripens unevenly with blotches**

☹ Spotted wilt virus.

☺ Remove infected plants and destroy. Spray healthy plants with CONFIDOR for thrips and aphid control. Remove weeds nearby.

6 **Yellowing of leaves at base of plant. Stems show brown discolouration if cut**

☹ Fusarium wilt.

☺ Prevalent in warm weather. Plant disease-resistant varieties, e.g. 'Summerstar', 'Big Beef' and 'Roma'. Practise crop rotation.

FRUIT

AVOCADO

1 Leaves wilt, yellow and die. Branches die back from tip

☹ Phytophthora root rot.

☺ Ensure good drainage. Avoid clay soils. Avoid overwatering.

Flowers fall

☹ Reduced fruit set.

☺ Avoid fertilising during flowering.

2 Small leaves, crowded with yellowing between veins

☹ Zinc deficiency.

☺ When actively growing, water foliage with THRIVE SOLUBLE ALL PURPOSE and apply YATES TRACE ELEMENTS MIX.

3 Leaves folded or webbed together. Chewed skin on fruit; forms brown scars

☹ Leaf roller caterpillar.

☺ Spray with TARGET or SUCCESS NATURALYTE.

4 Circular spots on fruit, which enlarge and darken. Rot spreads through flesh

☹ Anthracnose.

☺ Spores spread in warm, wet weather. Handle fruit carefully to avoid damage. Store in a cool, well-ventilated area. Spray with LIQUID COPPER at monthly intervals from flowering to harvest. Prune out dead twigs.

BLUEBERRY

1 Leaves rolled, folded and chewed

☹ Leaf roller caterpillar.

☺ Spray with NATURE'S WAY CATERPILLAR KILLER.

2 Chewed leaf edges in November and December. Defoliation of some plants

☹ Grass grub beetle.

☺ Spray with NATURE'S WAY PYRETHRUM.

3 Notches and holes chewed out of leaves. Dieback of plants

☹ Weevils.

☺ Apply DERRIS DUST.

4 Wilting of plant. Large numbers of insects which jump when disturbed

☹ Passion vine hopper.

☺ Spray with NATURE'S WAY PYRETHRUM. The adult passion vine hopper is very difficult to eradicate. Control is best achieved by spraying when the insects are in their juvenile stage, characterised by their fluffy white tail.

5 Black sooty mould on leaves and stems

☹ Sooty mould.

☺ Sooty mould lives on honeydew secreted by sucking insects. Spray with NATURE'S WAY PYRETHRUM.

6 Wilting of plant. Leaves distorted and puckered. Insects under leaves or on new growth

☹ Aphids.

☺ Spray with NATURE'S WAY PYRETHRUM or INSECT & MITE SPRAY.

Fruit

1   Wilting of leaves and dieback of twigs

☹ Scale.

☺ Hand remove by scrubbing with a gentle brush.

2   Stunting of plants. Galls on roots

☹ Nematodes.

☺ Remove infected plants. Plant in different area of garden.

BRAMBLE (BLACKBERRY, BOYSENBERRY, DEWBERRY, LOGANBERRY) (see also Raspberry)

3   Buds eaten and leaves emerge in tatters

☹ Raspberry bud moth.

☺ Prune as soon after picking as possible. Apply DERRIS DUST through growing season.

4   Hole in stem end of fruit. Grubs in fruit. Leaves rolled together

☹ Leaf roller caterpillar.

☺ Spray with NATURE'S WAY CATERPILLAR KILLER.

5   Leaves become stippled, yellow and dehydrated. Fine webbing is sometimes visible on underside of leaves

☹ Mites.

☺ Common in hot, dry weather. Spray with NATURE'S WAY INSECT & MITE SPRAY or MITE KILLER.

6   Leaves have purple or black patches. Stems develop purple patches. Fruit is deformed and shrivelled

☹ Dry berry, downy mildew.

☺ Spray with BRAVO.

7   Fruit develops a grey mould, becomes soft, watery and rots

☹ Botrytis, grey mould.

☺ Spray with BRAVO, particularly during flowering if rain is expected.

CITRUS (GRAPEFRUIT, LEMON, MANDARIN, ORANGE, TANGELO)

1 Clusters of black insects on young leaves

☹ Aphids.

☺ Keep plants well watered in dry weather. Spray with TARGET or NATURE'S WAY INSECT & MITE SPRAY.

2 Presence of black, sooty mould. Small, mealy insects found in protected cavities

☹ Mealybug.

☺ Spray with TARGET.

3 Poor growth, pale dehydrated leaves. Fruit small and dry. Hard, scale-like insects on woody and green stems

☹ Scale.

☺ Scale numbers quickly build up in dry seasons. Spray with TARGET or CONQUEROR OIL over summer.

4 Leaves tightly rolled and foliage and surface fruit eaten

☹ Leaf roller caterpillar.

☺ Spray with TARGET from October to March.

5 Snow-white, soft scale. Sooty mould present

☹ Soft wax scale.

☺ Spray with TARGET or CONQUEROR OIL over summer.

6 Silvering of foliage and fruit. Black spots of excrement may be seen

☹ Thrips.

☺ Spray with TARGET or CONQUEROR OIL over summer.

1 **Leaves yellow and dehydrated. Minute insects under leaves**

☹ Mites.

☺ Common in hot, dry weather. Spray with MITE KILLER or NATURE'S WAY INSECT & MITE SPRAY.

2 **Trees show poor growth, are dehydrated and branches die. Holes in branches and presence of 'sawdust'**

☹ Lemon tree borer.

☺ Prune out infected wood and burn. Spray into holes with NATURE'S WAY PYRETHRUM.

3 **Fruit develops brown rot and drops from the tree. The disease has a characteristic smell**

☹ Citrus brown rot.

☺ Prune out the lower branches of tree to increase air circulation. Spray with CHAMP DP.

4 **Splits and puckers in leaves**

☹ Wind damage causing new leaves to rub against branches or thorns.

☺ Shelter from strong winds.

5 **Pale, small leaves**

☹ Lack of fertiliser.

☺ Citrus are heavy feeders. Feed in spring and autumn with THRIVE CITRUS FOOD or ACTICOTE FRUIT, CITRUS, TREES & SHRUBS.

6 **Light green leaves fading to pale yellow or white. Veins remain green**

☹ Iron deficiency.

☺ Common in alkaline soils. Fertilise with THRIVE CITRUS FOOD, CHELATED IRON or SULPHATE OF IRON.

7 **Irregular, grey, scabby, wart-like growth on fruit or stems**

☹ Verrucosis, scab.

☺ Spray with COPPER OXYCHLORIDE or CHAMP DP.

1 **New leaves small and narrow, growing close together**

☹ Zinc deficiency.

☺ Spray foliage with THRIVE ALL PURPOSE PLANT FOOD. Apply YATES TRACE ELEMENTS MIX. Zinc is leached out of light, sandy soils and may be unavailable in highly alkaline soils.

2 **Spots on leaves, fruit and stems of mandarins**

☹ Brown spot.

☺ Common in cool, damp weather. Prune dead material and burn it. Spray with CHAMP DP.

3 **Older leaves yellow from outer edge**

☹ Magnesium deficiency.

☺ Liquid feed with THRIVE SOLUBLE FLOWER & FRUIT and fertilise regularly with THRIVE CITRUS FOOD.

4 **Small, dark, red-brown spots on leaves and fruit, often merging. Skin may crack**

☹ Melanose.

☺ More common on older trees in warm, humid weather. Prune off dead twigs and branches. Spray with CHAMP DP or COPPER OXYCHLORIDE at monthly intervals.

CURRANT

Shoots and stems wilt and die due to hollowing-out by boring insect

☹ Currant borer.

☺ Remove and burn infected parts.

5 **Leaves rolled together**

☹ Leaf roller caterpillar.

☺ Spray with NATURE'S WAY CATERPILLAR SPRAY.

Fruit

93

FEIJOA

1 **Poor growth. Dehydrated leaves. Hard, scale-like insects on woody and green stems**

☹ Scale.

☺ Scale numbers build up quickly in dry seasons. Keep well watered and hand remove infestations.

2 **Leaves rolled or stuck together. Surface of fruit eaten**

☹ Leaf roller caterpillar.

☺ Remove affected leaves. Spray with NATURE'S WAY CATERPILLAR KILLER.

3 **Leaves yellow (stippled or mottled), becoming dehydrated. Fine webbing present on undersides of leaves**

☹ Mites.

☺ Spray with NATURE'S WAY INSECT & MITE SPRAY.

FIG

4 **Soft dark patches on fruit, developing into mouldy rot.**

☹ Botrytis fungus.

☺ Remove and bin infected fruit.

5 **Holes in fruit, fruit rotting**

☹ Wasp damage.

☺ Remove and bin infected fruit.

6 **Fruit not ripening**

☹ Lack of water or nutrients.

☺ Keep well watered during fruit production. Fertilise annually with DYNAMIC LIFTER PLUS FRUIT FOOD or ACTICOTE FRUIT, CITRUS TREES & SHRUBS.

7 **Small pecks in fruit**

☹ Bird damage.

☺ Spread bird netting over tree before fruit begins to ripen.

Tree not thriving

☹ Too wet or shaded.

☺ Transplant into well drained soil in warm, sunny position.

1 Brown spots on leaves with orange pustules on underside.

☹ Rust.

☺ Spray with NATURE'S WAY FUNGUS SPRAY.

2 Tree not fruiting

☹ Too shaded, too much nitrogen or lack of nutrients.

☺ Transplant to warm, sunny area. Fertilise annually with DYNAMIC LIFTER PLUS FRUIT FOOD or ACTICOTE FRUIT, CITRUS TREES & SHRUBS.

GOOSEBERRY

3 Brown spots on leaves

☹ Leaf spot.

☺ Spray with LIQUID COPPER.

4 Silver appearance of leaves. Poor growth

☹ Silver leaf.

☺ Cut out infected wood and burn. Prune in dry weather. Seal cuts with BACSEAL PRUNING PAINT.

5 Leaves develop a spreading white mould

☹ Powdery mildew.

☺ Spray with NATURE'S WAY FUNGUS SPRAY.

GRAPE

6 Young leaves webbed together and eaten. Fruit shrivels

☹ Leaf roller caterpillar.

☺ Spray with NATURE'S WAY CATERPILLAR KILLER.

Fruit

1   **Black spots on stems and leaves**

🙁 Black spot.

☺ Common in cool, damp weather. Spray with GREENGUARD or NATURE'S WAY FUNGUS SPRAY.

2   **Yellow or brown irregular spots on leaves. Brown spots on fruit. A grey-brown mould develops under leaves**

🙁 Downy mildew.

☺ Worst in warm or humid conditions. Avoid overhead watering. Prune to minimise shaded, moist pockets. Spray regularly with NATURE'S WAY FUNGUS SPRAY or LIQUID COPPER.

3   **White, powdery film on leaves and fruit. Mouldy smell**

🙁 Powdery mildew.

☺ Common in warm weather. Spray with GREENGUARD, FUNGUS FIGHTER or LIQUID COPPER.

4   **Fruit develops a grey-brown mould and rots**

🙁 Botrytis, grey mould.

☺ Most prevalent in warm, wet weather late in the season. Spray with GREENGUARD, particularly at flowering to prevent later development.

5   **Weak growth. Reduced crops. Leaves may have irregular swellings on lower surface**

🙁 Phylloxera aphid.

☺ Vines in heavy clay soils are more susceptible to this. Destroy infected plants. Grow grapes on resistant root stock.

6   **No fruit set. Leaves turn red-brown prematurely. Stunted appearance**

🙁 Virus.

☺ Destroy plant.

GUAVA

1 Fruit develop roughened areas and become hard. Leaves silver and dehydrated

☹ Thrips.

☺ Most common in dry weather. Keep well watered. Spray with NATURE'S WAY FRUIT & VEGIE GUN.

KIWIFRUIT

2 Leaves folded or rolled together. Fruit skin chewed

☹ Leaf roller caterpillar.

☺ Spray with SUCCESS NATURALYTE or NATURE'S WAY CATERPILLAR KILLER.

3 Chewed leaf edges, mostly in November and December

☹ Grass grub beetle.

☺ Spray with NATURE'S WAY PYRETHRUM.

4 Ragged notching of leaves

☹ Weevil.

☺ Cultivate soil after harvest to expose pupation cells at soil surface.

5 Sticky honeydew on which sooty mould may grow

☹ Passion vine hopper.

☺ Spray with NATURE'S WAY PYRETHRUM.

6 Small insects feeding on new growth, causing distortion

☹ Aphids.

☺ Spray with NATURE'S WAY PYRETHRUM or INSECT & MITE SPRAY.

7 White fluffy insects present

☹ Mealybug.

☺ Spray with NATURE'S WAY PYRETHRUM.

Fruit

1 **Small brown scale. Plant does not thrive. Dimples on fruit. Tips of twigs die back**

☹ Scale.

☺ Scale numbers build up quickly in dry seasons. Replace with: Spray with LIME SULFUR in winter.

2 **Bronzing of leaves with webbing on undersides**

☹ Mites.

☺ Spray with MITE KILLER or NATURE'S WAY INSECT & MITE SPRAY.

LOQUAT

Juvenile plants wilt

☹ Phytophthora root rot.

☺ Soil too wet. Plant in a free-draining soil.

3 **Black spots or scabs on leaves and fruit**

☹ Black spot.

☺ Select resistant strains. Spray with NATURE'S WAY FUNGUS SPRAY.

4 **Leaves become blackened, particularly in cool, wet weather**

☹ Fire blight (bacterial disease).

☺ Remove infected wood and burn. Spray with NATURE'S WAY FUNGUS SPRAY.

OLIVE

Fruit not ripening

☹ Incorrect climate.

☺ Olives require a frost-free climate with sufficient winter chill to set the fruit and long, hot summer to ripen the fruit.

5 **Leaves yellowing, defoliation, bare growth tips followed by die back of branches.**

☹ Phytophthora root rot.

☺ Destroy infected trees. Plant in well-drained soil.

1. **Brown patches on fruit and leaf tip burn.**
   ☹ Frost damage.
   ☺ Protect from frost. Plant earlier fruiting varieties.

2. **Small raised, brown lumps on stems.**
   ☹ Scale insect.
   ☺ Hand remove with a gentle brush.

PASSIONFRUIT

Young plants eaten
   ☹ Slugs or snails.
   ☺ Protect with BLITZEM or BAYSOL.

3. **Insects in clusters on young leaves**
   ☹ Aphids.
   ☺ Water regularly in dry weather. Spray with NATURE'S WAY INSECT & MITE SPRAY or PYRETHRUM.

4. **Presence of black, sooty mould. Small, mealy insects found close to stems and protected cavities**
   ☹ Mealybug.
   ☺ Hand remove with a gentle brush.

5. **Leaves eaten**
   ☹ Caterpillars.
   ☺ Spray with NATURE'S WAY CATERPILLAR KILLER.

6. **Brown spots on leaves and fruit**
   ☹ Septoria spot or brown spot.
   ☺ Spray with CHAMP DP.

7. **Small insects which jump when disturbed**
   ☹ Passion vine hopper.
   ☺ Spray with NATURE'S WAY PYRETHRUM.

Fruit

1 **Woodiness of fruit. Rind is very thick with small fruit cavity. Leaves may be mottled**

☹ Virus disease carried by aphids.

☺ Control insects. Replace vines every three to five years.

2 **Fruit, leaves and stems develop a grey mould and rot**

☹ Botrytis, grey mould.

☺ Most common in wet or humid weather. Spray with NATURE'S WAY FUNGUS SPRAY.

3 **Brown patches on mature leaves and fruit, and shoots may die from the tips**

☹ Phytophthora root rot.

☺ Destroy plant. Replant in well-drained soil in different area of garden.

Plants wilt, collapse and die

☹ Fusarium root rot, crown rot.

☺ Plant in well-drained soil. Avoid replanting in same position.

4 **Raised, rough, wet or greasy lesions on fruit. Wilting and dying of stems. Fruit shrivels and falls**

☹ Grease spot, bacterial spot.

☺ More common in wet weather. Don't grow in heavy soils. No effective control.

PERSIMMON

5 **White, cottony insects**

☹ Mealybug.

☺ Hand remove severe infestations.

6 **Leaves wilt, yellow and die**

☹ Phytophthora root rot.

☺ Plant only in well-drained soil. Avoid clay soils. Avoid overwatering.

Fruit not forming

☹ Plant too young.

☺ Plants may take some years to fruit.

1 Small brown discs attached to leaves and stems

☹ Scale.

☺ Spray with LIME SULFUR in winter.

2 Tiny black insects feeding on underside of leaves, silvering foliage

☹ Thrips.

☺ Spray with NATURE'S WAY FRUIT & VEGIE GUN.

PIPFRUIT (APPLE, PEAR, QUINCE)

3 Insects clustered on new growth

☹ Aphids.

☺ Spray with NATURE'S WAY INSECT & MITE SPRAY or PYRETHRUM.

4 Tightly rolled leaves on young shoots, which may be pink in colour

☹ Leaf curling midge.

☺ Damage most severe on young trees. The fly overwinters as a pupa in the soil. Prune and destroy galls from infested plants. Remove badly infested plants.

5 Tunnels in fruit

☹ Codling moth.

☺ Destroy infested fruit. Remove flaking bark from tree trunks. Some larvae can be trapped by placing cardboard around trunk. Hang codling moth traps from October onwards.

6 Leaves rolled, folded or webbed. Fruit is blemished

☹ Leaf roller caterpillar.

☺ Spray with SUCCESS NATURALYTE.

Fruit

1 **Leaves become yellow (stippled or mottled) and dehydrated in hot weather. Minute insects under leaves**

☹ Mites.

☺ Spray with CONQUEROR OIL in late winter to control eggs. Spray with MITE KILLER or NATURE'S WAY INSECT & MITE SPRAY over summer.

2 **Black spots on leaves and fruit**

☹ Black spot, scab.

☺ A wet-weather disease. Destroy all leaves in autumn. Spray with LIQUID COPPER in winter or apply LIME SULFUR during bud movement stage. Spray regularly with FUNGUS FIGHTER from bud break to fruit set.

3 **New growing tips die. Gum is produced around the twig**

☹ Oriental fruit moth.

☺ Cut off and burn infested twigs. Wrap cardboard or hessian around trunk to trap larvae. Remove infested fruit every few days. Remove loose bark and rubbish at base of tree.

4 **Areas of dead bark cracking in rings, often completely around a branch**

☹ European canker.

☺ Remove and burn diseased wood. Spray with COPPER OXYCHLORIDE at leaf fall.

5 **White, powdery mould on leaves, particularly the young growing tips. Fruit develops with yellowish criss-crossing lines on skins**

☹ Powdery mildew.

☺ Spray regularly with FUNGUS FIGHTER.

6 **Dark brown spots on ripening fruit**

☹ Glomerella or ripe spot.

☺ Remove and destroy all mummified fruit at pruning to prevent carryover of spores. Prune out cankers and dead wood in winter.

1 **Water-soaked spots on fruit skin. Pits turn brown and become dry and spongy**

☹ Bitter pit (calcium deficiency).

☺ Occurs more on young trees. Apply GRO-PLUS LIME to raise soil pH to 6.5–6.8.

2 **Fruit cracks. Rough skin and dark, spongy areas in fruit**

☹ Boron deficiency.

☺ Avoid fluctuations in soil moisture. Spray with THRIVE LIQUID ALL PURPOSE PLANT FOOD.

3 **Chewed leaf edges**

☹ Bronze beetle, grass grub beetle.

☺ Spray with NATURE'S WAY PYRETHRUM.

4 **Leaves become blackened and die back**

☹ Fire blight (bacterial disease).

☺ Trees with vigorous growth are more susceptible — keep vigour under control. Keep weeds down. Remove and burn infected wood. Remove cankers in winter. Spray with COPPER OXYCHLORIDE. Protect wounds with BACSEAL PRUNING PAINT.

5 **Yellow-green hopping insects that feed by sucking plant sap, producing white areas**

☹ Leaf hopper.

☺ Spray with NATURE'S WAY PYRETHRUM, or use sticky traps.

6 **Leaf surface removed with only veins left (pear only)**

☹ Cherry slug.

☺ Spray with NATURE'S WAY PYRETHRUM or SUCCESS NATURALYTE.

7 **Sooty mould**

☹ Sucking insects secrete honeydew on which mould grows.

☺ Winter spray with LIME SULFUR to control scale insects.

Fruit

1 Scarlet spotting on fruit
☹ San Jose scale.
☺ Spray with CONQUEROR OIL in winter.

Marked skin
☹ Oyster shell scale.
☺ Spray with CONQUEROR OIL in winter and CONFIDOR and CONQUEROR OIL (mixed together) in summer.

2 Lumps and scars on twigs, with white, cottony masses
☹ Woolly aphid.
☺ Plant modern resistant varieties.

RASPBERRY (see also Bramble)

No fruit
☹ Incorrect pruning.
☺ Remove old canes only, leave young canes intact.

3 Yellow pustules on leaves which later turn black
☹ Rust.
☺ Spray with NATURE'S WAY FUNGUS SPRAY at first sign of infection.

4 Buds eaten out. Shoots emerge in tatters
☹ Raspberry bud moth.
☺ Prune as soon after fruiting as possible. Spray with NATURE'S WAY PYRETHRUM over spring and summer.

Wilting and dying back of cane
☹ Cane wilt.
☺ Remove and burn old fruiting canes and infected young canes. Spray with CHAMP DP at green tip stage.

1 **Spots on canes and leaves.**
   Canes may crack
   ☹ Cane spot.
   ☺ Prune out and burn infected canes. Avoid
   overcrowding. Spray with CHAMP DP.

2 **Berries hard, dry and split.**
   Leaves have pinkish blotches
   ☹ Dryberry, downy mildew.
   ☺ Spray with BRAVO.

RHUBARB

3 **Brown rot at base of plant**
   ☹ Crown rot.
   ☺ Improve drainage and ensure crown of plant
   not buried.

   Wilting and death of plant
   ☹ Sclerotinia.
   ☺ Destroy plants. Replant into well-drained soil
   using YATES ORGANIC SOIL CONDITIONER
   (WORMICAST).

4 **Yellowish spots on leaves with rust-**
   coloured pustules on lower surface
   ☹ Rust.
   ☺ Destroy infected leaves. Spray with NATURE'S
   WAY FUNGUS SPRAY at first sign of infection.

5 **Small brown spots on leaves which go red,**
   brown or black
   ☹ Leaf spot.
   ☺ Plant in sunny, well-drained location; keep
   weeds down. Keep plants growing vigorously in
   spring. Remove and destroy all infected leaves
   and plant debris. Spray with NATURE'S WAY
   FUNGUS SPRAY.

6 **Angular, light brown patches.**
   Furry growth on underside of leaves
   ☹ Downy mildew.
   ☺ Remove and burn infected leaves. Spray with
   NATURE'S WAY FUNGUS SPRAY.

Fruit

STONEFRUIT (APRICOT, CHERRY, NECTARINE, PEACH, PLUM)

1 **Leaves emerge deformed and blistered, usually pink or yellow in colour**

☹ Leaf curl.

☺ Spray with BRAVO, NATURE'S WAY FUNGUS SPRAY or LIQUID COPPER at leaf bud swell in early spring.

2 **Leaves yellowing in spots. Orange or red pustules on undersides of leaves in summer and autumn**

☹ Rust.

☺ Spray with NATURE'S WAY FUNGUS SPRAY, or apply LIME SULFUR at bud movement.

3 **Small brown spots that dry out and leave clean, round holes. Fruit may have scabs and skin cracks. Gum exudes from twigs**

☹ Shot hole.

☺ Spray with NATURE'S WAY FUNGUS SPRAY or LIQUID COPPER.

4 **Fruit develops a brown rot, which spreads quickly through the fruit when it approaches maturity. Trees sometimes exude gum**

☹ Brown rot.

☺ Spray during flowering with BRAVO or GREENGUARD.

5 **Leaves turn a silvery grey colour and growth slows**

☹ Silver leaf.

☺ Most common in areas with mild, wet winters. Remove and burn infected branches. Prune only on dry days and sterilise secateurs thoroughly. Seal pruning cuts with BACSEAL PRUNING PAINT.

1 **Swollen, distorted, empty fruit**

☹ Bladder plum.

☺ Infected shoots should be removed during growing season. Spray with CHAMP DP at bud swelling.

2 **Circular, water-soaked spots with dark centres; margins of large lesions that become raised**

☹ Bacterial spot.

☺ Spray with COPPER OXYCHLORIDE.

3 **Distortion and rapid dieback of growing tips. Blackening of stems. Spots or scabs on leaves and fruit. Trees may exude gum**

☹ Stone fruit blast.

☺ Actively growing trees are resistant. Fertilise regularly with DYNAMIC LIFTER PLUS FRUIT FOOD. Prune out infected tissue. Spray with COPPER OXYCHLORIDE.

Insects clustered on young leaves

☹ Aphids.

☺ Spray with NATURE'S WAY INSECT & MITE SRPAY or GUARDALL.

4 **Young leaves webbed together and eaten**

☹ Leaf roller caterpillar.

☺ Spray with TARGET or SUCCESS NATURALYTE.

5 **Young growing tips wither and die back. Boring insect found in terminal shoots and in fruit**

☹ Oriental fruit moth.

☺ Cut off and burn infested twigs. Wrap cardboard or hessian around trunk to trap larvae. Remove infested fruit every few days. Remove loose bark and rubbish at base of tree.

6 **Leaves eaten and left as transparent skeletons. Black slug-like insects present**

☹ Cherry and pear slug.

☺ Spray with NATURE'S WAY PYRETHRUM or SUCCESS NATURALYTE.

Fruit

1 Leaves yellow (stippled) and dehydrated, particularly in hot, dry weather. Minute pests under leaves

☹ Mites.

☺ Spray with MITE KILLER or CONQUEROR OIL.

2 Silvering of foliage. Scarring and distortion on fruit skin

☹ Thrips.

☺ Spray with NATURE'S WAY FRUIT & VEGIE GUN at flowering.

STRAWBERRY

3 Insects clustered on new leaves, causing foliage distortion

☹ Aphids.

☺ Spray on appearance with NATURE'S WAY PYRETHRUM or INSECT & MITE SPRAY.

4 Leaves stippled yellow or rusty brown in colour. Fine webbing and reddish mites on undersides of leaves

☹ Mites.

☺ Most common in hot, dry weather. Spray at first appearance in early spring with MITE KILLER or NATURE'S WAY INSECT & MITE SPRAY.

Plants cease to thrive and do not crop. Roots diseased and rotting

☹ Verticillium and other soil-borne fungal diseases.

☺ Destroy plants. Replace soil with fresh soil or grow in containers. Always plant in well-drained, well-composted soil.

5 Leaves develop brown or black spots

☹ Leaf spot.

☺ More prevalent in humid weather. Water plants when quick drying of leaves and fruit is possible. Pick fruit thoroughly. Spray with BRAVO or LIQUID COPPER.

1 Fruit develops grey mould and rots

☹ Botrytis, grey mould.

☺ More prevalent in wet weather. Pick off and destroy infected fruit. Spray with BRAVO or LIQUID COPPER.

TAMARILLO

2 Holes in leaves

☹ Caterpillars.

☺ Spray regularly with NATURE'S WAY PYRETHRUM.

3 Tiny white insects on undersides of leaves which fly when disturbed

☹ Whitefly.

☺ Spray with NATURE'S WAY PYRETHRUM or CATERPILLAR KILLER.

4 White, powdery mould starting in spots and spreading over the leaf. Leaf develops black patches, turns yellow, then drops off

☹ Powdery mildew.

☺ Spray with NATURE'S WAY FUNGUS SPRAY in spring to catch the first infection and then at two- to three-week intervals. Prune to increase air movement through plants.

INDEX

NOTES

Otaika Valley
School